JOURNEY TO SOLD

GEOFF GRIST

JOURNEY TO SOLD

Your Passport to a Profitable Property Sale

Praise for *Journey to Sold*

'Selling real estate is a complex process with lots of small steps along the way, so I love that Geoff has broken down the real estate journey to help educate sellers of the importance of working with a great real estate agent who will guide you through the maze of selling. Following Geoff's tips will help you sell for top dollar in the fastest possible time.

Aaron Shiner, Co-founder of LockedOn

'Once again, Geoff has shown us why he is one of Australasia's leading real estate agents and business owners. He has a unique way of telling a compelling story and an outstanding ability to have those who work with him embrace and follow his example. His knowledge and understanding of what it takes to successfully sell a property is cleverly laid out in this book. Anyone can sell a property, but not every agent does it well. This book sets the benchmark for all real estate agents and clearly shows why it is not easy to sell a property well.'

Kevin Turner, CEO and Lead Anchor at Property.TV

'The role of an agent is to anticipate the unmet, unidentified and unsatisfied needs of today's ever-changing customer. A great agent takes the pressure off the client. It's the agent's systems, methodology and approach that generates exceptional results. I've known Geoff for over 12 years, and this book is a testament to his detailed knowledge and aspiration to improve our industry.'

Josh Phegan, Speaker - Trainer - Coach at joshphegan.com.au

‘In *Journey to Sold*, Geoff Grist illustrates his meticulous, intelligent, proven and highly successful approach to selling property. It is so refreshing to read the words of someone who is not only a lateral thinker, but a person who holds such a high position of respect within the property industry. This book finds the solutions, gives the correct answers and is a must-read for anyone contemplating the biggest financial transaction of their lifetime.’

Peter Baldwin, Director/Chief Auctioneer, Richardson & Wrench Pty Limited

‘Great insight from a trusted source. An easy-to-understand, invaluable reference for anyone looking to sell their property, from a seasoned property professional. Well worth the read.’

Ben Dickson, Exclusive Buyers Agent at Hunter Manor

‘Every real estate sale is a journey for the seller. Naturally, there’s a lot at stake. The critical difference with property is that it has no recommended retail price, which means that every seller, armed with the right advice, information and support, has the opportunity to influence their selling price to achieve a top market result. There would be few people better qualified than Geoff Grist to guide sellers through the real estate selling journey, and *Journey to Sold* pulls back the curtain on everything required to deliver not only a great selling price, but also a rewarding real estate selling experience. From preparation, to launching the marketing campaign, to negotiating the best result, *Journey to Sold* lays out a proven road map for success from someone who knows the process backwards. Don’t do this alone. Discover the powerful edge Geoff’s knowledge and experience will give to your next sale.’

Ray Wood, CEO, Bestagents Australia & New Zealand

'I work with real estate agents at all times in their careers and am always reminding them to "systemise for success". I have had the pleasure of working with Geoff and he has gone above and beyond to "write it down" to help educate property sellers and raise the bar for his peers in the real estate industry. This book helps demystify the sales process so that sellers better understand the value their agents deliver.'

Robert Williams, Real Estate Trainer/Coach and Mentor at www.mrlister.com.au

'Whether you are selling your home for the first time, or have sold many homes, Geoff has great advice and takeaways right here in this book. It's like Wikipedia for home selling – a step-by-step guide with something for absolutely everyone.'

Samantha McLean, Managing Editor, Elite Agent

'There is a saying that every journey begins with a first step. Many people find the journey of selling their home to be stressful, confusing and complex, and often don't know where to start or what to do. Real estate expert Geoff Grist has produced a masterful summary of how to sell your home that will assist every seller in navigating this challenging process. Drawing upon his many years of producing outstanding results for his clients, Geoff has been able to crystallise his experience in a clear, logical and easy-to-read road map of the path to a successful sale. If you're considering embarking on the journey of selling your home, your first step should be to buy this book.'

Andrew Cocks, Owner and Managing Director, Richardson & Wrench Group

First published in 2019 by Major Street Publishing Pty Ltd
PO Box 106, Highett, Vic. 3190 E: info@majorstreet.com.au
W: majorstreet.com.au M: +61 421 707 983

Quantity sales. Special discounts are available on quantity purchases by corporations, associations and others. For details, contact Lesley Williams using the contact details above.

Individual sales. Major Street publications are available through most bookstores. They can also be ordered directly from Major Street's online bookstore at www.majorstreet.com.au.

Orders for university textbook/course adoption use. For orders of this nature, please contact Lesley Williams using the contact details above.

NATIONAL LIBRARY OF AUSTRALIA

A catalogue record for this book is available from the National Library of Australia

ISBN: 978-0-6485159-3-7

Cover design by Simone Geary
Internal design by Production Works

10 9 8 7 6 5 4 3 2 1

CONTENTS

1. GETTING STARTED

STEP 1 – PREPARING FOR TAKE-OFF

You have decided to sell your home or investment property and you want what every property seller wants - the best advice to enjoy a rewarding real estate experience to achieve top dollar in a reasonable timeframe. Only a great real estate agent can meet your needs, in much the same way as working with a great travel agent can deliver a more rewarding holiday experience than you can get by making the arrangements yourself.

Think of a great real estate agent as the project manager for your *Journey to Sold.* Selling your greatest asset is a process-driven activity that requires a broad range of experience to anticipate the pitfalls ahead and navigate you safely to your final destination. You may be surprised at how many things can and will go wrong during your sale, so choosing a great real estate agent is like travel insurance for a safe and profitable journey.

Your real estate journey is specific to you: each property seller will find a slightly different way to get to their final destination.

You can choose to travel economy, premium, business, first class or even private charter. You can also choose your level of accommodation, from backpacker's hostels or one- and two-star accommodation, right up to five-star luxury resorts. As with all things in life, you will get what you pay for and, if you want a better experience and a higher level of service, then your choice of real estate agent will determine your level of comfort throughout your journey.

Your property sale is just like planning your world trip:

1. You need to decide when to depart and return, or when you need to be sold by, and when you need to be in your new home. What are your critical dates?
2. What's your final destination? Where are you going to move to after you sell?
3. What's your budget? Are you travelling as a backpacker or first-class passenger? How much are you prepared to invest in the success of your sale?
4. Have you done your online research? You need to do your homework on how you will travel – in other words, how you will sell.
5. You need to choose the right 'travel agent'. Who's the right real estate agent for you?

6. Your method of travel might be car, train, ship or aeroplane. Your method of sale might be auction, private treaty or expressions of interest.
7. You have to be prepared. You can't leave home without your passport, the right visas and an itinerary. Equally, you can't expect buyers to fall in love with your home without some preparation.
8. You need to pack your bags to leave on your journey and pack your emotions to start your sale.
9. Departure day for your trip is like the first day your home is on the market. Can you believe the day is finally here!

As your project manager, your real estate agent will work with you and find out what type of traveller you are. Do you expect a champagne holiday on a beer budget, or will you pay for great service and a great result with the possibility of some upgrades along the way?

Not all real estate agents are the same, just as not all travel agents are the same. Some travel agents will simply offer you the packaged holiday from a brochure; they haven't been there themselves, but it's a package so what can go wrong? Elite travel agents understand your needs and add immense value from all their own experiences, so they can offer you an extraordinary and memorable holiday.

So which travel agent do you want to work with - the package-deal salesperson or the one offering the tailored itinerary?

And which real estate agent do you believe will deliver the results you deserve?

You can choose to book your once-in-a-lifetime, round-- the-world trip on the internet yourself and if you do, all I can say is good luck with that. You don't know what you don't know, so booking your trip yourself will cost you more than just money. It will also cost you time and a whole range of emotions from anxiety to depression when you find yourself stranded in a foreign country with no one to help you. I know of a family who booked and paid in advance for an overseas hotel online, and when they arrived, the hotel address was a vacant carpark. The website looked genuine and the photos were detailed but the whole thing was a scam. They had been tricked out of a substantial sum of money and were stranded, physically and emotionally.

Alternatively, you could choose to book your once-in-a-lifetime, round-the-world trip with an elite travel agent, who not only has the expertise to understand what you expect from a great travel experience, but also has access to upgrades and benefits that are an exclusive part of their service offering.

Travel can be a risky business, but you can minimise your risk by making logical (not emotional) decisions that will all but guarantee a wonderful experience.

Real estate agents offer different levels of competence and experience as well, so it is important to make a business decision to engage the right real estate agent as the project manager for your property sale. Leave your emotional baggage at the door and make a business decision.

Hopefully, the information in this book will help you understand the entire sales process so you do choose the right real estate agent to make your *Journey to Sold* both rewarding and profitable.

STEP 2 – PLANNING AHEAD

Have you ever noticed that flights are cheaper when they are first released and become more expensive the closer you get to the departure date?

As with any journey, you need to plan ahead to embark on your trip of a lifetime. The same goes for selling a property. Your journey starts with one first step, and that is to hire the very best project manager possible to be your licensed real estate agent for your entire journey.

Project management is defined in part by Wikipedia as:

> *... the practice of initiating, planning, executing, controlling and closing the work of a team to achieve specific goals and meet specific success criteria at the specified time. A project is a temporary endeavour designed to produce a unique product, service or result with a defined beginning and end undertaken to meet unique goals and objectives, typically to bring about beneficial change or added value.*

With this definition in mind, I will share with you throughout this book how my real estate team deliver on our promise to project manage your sale. The same level of service and results I deliver for my clients will be what you want from your real estate agent as well. While I can't tell you what another agent may or may not do, I can tell you what I do now, which will give you an idea of what you should expect from any agent.

My home suburb is Mosman in Sydney, so the way I do things complies with the laws of New South Wales. While legislation and ways of doing things may be different where you are, the concepts will be similar. For brevity, I have often referred to anyone selling as a 'seller' rather than a 'vendor', and anyone buying as a 'buyer' rather than a 'purchaser'. Where possible, I refer to all solicitors, lawyers and conveyancers just as 'conveyancers', because that is the job they all do in real estate. While I have tried to avoid using industry jargon, I have compiled a useful glossary at the back of the book for you to refer to if you come across a term that you are not familiar with.

2. READY, SET, GO

STEP 1 – MEET EACH OTHER

The best way to describe the sales journey to you is to take you down the road with me as if you were to list your property with me. I am confident you will find it a surprising and fascinating journey, one that is definitely more complicated than you would imagine. So, let's get started.

It begins with a phone call. Most sellers call me when they are ready to talk, but sometimes I might call you at the exact right moment when you are ready to move forward.

On the first call, we will cover off the basics about where you are now and where you want to be. You will also give me a brief description of your property so I can complete my background sales information, which we will discuss in person at our first face-to-face meeting.

If meeting in person isn't possible after our first call, then I will put together a comprehensive online presentation.

This will be packed with useful information to help you determine the price range where your property should sit to attract willing buyers. I will email this to you for further discussion on the phone.

In most cases, though, I will source the initial background information on your property and set up a meeting in a day or two at the property so I can meet all the decision-makers. Properties can be owned by just one person, two people (often partners or husbands and wives) or several people (family members or investors), or they may even be in a company name. Properties can be purchased as joint tenants, tenants in common (see the glossary) or in unequal shares.

When I arrive at your home and before we sit down, it is the perfect opportunity for you to show me through the home. I will ask questions and make notes and will walk through the home much as a buyer will do at an inspection time. No question is off limits, because the more I know about your home, the better I can connect to buyers using the small details that make your house a home. Together we will review your property. I will be asking questions such as, 'Does it present as the type of home you would buy?', 'How does your home feel?' and 'Does it feel like you would want to buy it?'

I will also ask whether you have plans available for extensions or additions, or if have you ever lodged a development application (DA) or have had plans approved by council to build additions but have never started. Many home sellers have a DA approved. These may have a three- to five-year approval window and can often be locked in indefinitely by undertaking 'substantial commencement', which may not be as onerous as it sounds. Your agent should be made aware of any plans you have and should be able to advise you of the potential value of your DA to the right buyer.

Every home has a story to tell, too, and I want to hear the stories that will resonate most with buyers. It could be a story about a huge birthday party, or Christmas celebrations that you have hosted at the home for the extended family. Entertaining in your home is a shared family value that is so important to buyers. I want to know what it is that is unique to your home, what made you buy it and why you have stayed so long.

Every meeting needs an agenda to ensure we discuss everything and keep on track. After I listen to your story, most sellers want to discuss the following points:

1. Current market activity
2. Homes like theirs that I have sold recently
3. The method of sale I recommend and why
4. How I find and negotiate with buyers
5. The right price range that will create buyer interest to make their home sell
6. The investment they will need to make to market their home
7. Our success fee
8. Next steps.

It seems all sellers want the same thing. Everyone wants the highest price in a reasonable timeframe, wrapped up in a rewarding real estate sales experience with the least stress and lowest fees. Unfortunately, not all real estate agents are the same, so your experience will depend on whether you choose an experienced real estate agent, not the cheapest agent you can find. A great agent doesn't need to and generally won't discount their fees, because they will sell your home for a price that you would otherwise not have achieved if you used a lesser agent or tried to sell it yourself.

STEP 2 – THE JOB INTERVIEW

The meeting between agent and owners is in fact just like a job interview, so all decision-makers should be present. You will be interviewing me for the job of selling your property and I will be interviewing you to see that we are a good fit.

When you interview a real estate agent, are you looking to hire the very best agent to manage the process of selling your home, or you are looking for the cheapest agent to sell your home? The best agent will not be the cheapest agent and the cheapest agent certainly will not be the best.

Choose your real estate agent based on their competency and ability to demonstrate their strategy and process. Whatever selling fee they are asking will represent good value for the services they provide. You can't buy a new Mercedes for the price of a Honda, so it's best not to try and compare your chosen agent's fee with the fee of a lesser agent.

Real estate is not a job, it's a lifestyle. Agents exchange their time and services for money, but are only paid when they successfully sell your home for a price you are delighted with. No other professional service provider would offer you a deal like that. Your agent may have been working with a buyer for six months without getting paid before they list your home and know it's exactly what that buyer wants. It may feel to you as if it only took your agent a few days to put the deal together when in fact it's been months in the making.

Great agents are not discount agents and they do not offer limited or partial services - I'm sure you wouldn't be satisfied with a partially successful sale either! Great real estate agents are dedicated and hard working, with an unceasing commitment to delivering results that exceed your property expectations. Your agent does not get paid unless they sell your home for a price you are delighted to accept. Even then, they split the commission with their agency office and have their own expenses and taxes to pay, so in every sense of the word, your agent will earn their fee - and, despite what some people jokingly say, your property will not sell itself.

What makes a great real estate agent? Our clients have told us that:

1. They are attracted by our positive personality, strength of character and our determination.
2. We are humble, likeable and enthusiastic and have a heart, so we are empathetic.
3. We have broad life experiences and have adapted to change and achieved our goals.

4. We demonstrate balance and respond effectively and confidently, not forcefully.
5. We are customer focused, highly organised and we work well under pressure.

Great real estate agents have a passion for life, are good listeners and communicators, plus they set goals through processes with a determined understanding of the risk that is ever present in the real estate business. They work hand in hand with people at the most highly emotive time of their life.

Your real estate journey will be so much more rewarding with an experienced agent by your side, particularly when something goes wrong - and it will go wrong. There is no such thing as the perfect house and no such thing as the perfect sale; however, you will remember the bitterness of a bad experience for so much longer if it's the result of paying a cheap fee to the wrong agent. Having a great agent who is professional, ethical and a true advocate - who will ensure everything is taken care of and done properly to protect your interest - is invaluable to the success of your journey.

At our 'interview', I will cover everything you need to know to make your decision. We will have ample time to discuss any questions you may have, and I will provide answers, so that at the conclusion of the meeting we will have covered all aspects of the sale and the process. I will then ask you to sign the agency sales agreement. If you have decided that I am the agent to take you on this journey, then we will get started.

In my previous book, *Sold Above Market*, I devoted more than half of the book to the subject of choosing the right real estate agent, so I am not going to spend that time again in this book. The reason I covered that subject in such depth was that 2013 research from idashboard.com.au showed that '67% of people selling their property said choosing an agent was the most stressful step in the selling process'. I am told that *Sold Above Market* helped thousands of sellers to make a better decision. (Please see details at the back of the book about how to get hold of a copy of *Sold Above Market*.)

Selling real estate can be a roller-coaster ride and your agent needs to overcome road-blocks from buyers, and manage feedback and obstacles to stay the path. I do this by asking lots of questions of buyers to extract as much information as I can from their current situation, so I can help them move to the next stage. I know that when a sale stalls, it's my responsibility and I need to know the steps to take to get it back on track.

STEP 3 – SIGNING THE AGENCY SALES AGREEMENT

We use the standard Real Estate Institute of NSW Sales Inspection Report and Agency Agreement. There are two versions: one is an Auction Agency Agreement and the other is an Exclusive Sales Agreement (Private Treaty or For Sale Agreement).

The agency sales agreement gives me your permission to sell your property. I can't sell your home without it, as it defines all the things we have agreed on to effect the sale, including the price and the fee. The agreement sets out details around the following headlines:

- *Parties* - Your details as the Principal and our details as the Agent
- *Property* - Address of the property for sale, together with the inclusions specified in the contract; any covenants, easements or notices; whether the property is offered with vacant possession or subject to existing tenancies; and any special conditions specified in the contract
- *Price* - The Agent's opinion of estimated selling price and your instructions to the Agent to market the property at a price guide
- *Method* - The recommended method of sale (also determined by the document type)
- *Conveyancer* - Your legal representative's full details
- *Agency period* - Date of commencement and finish
- *Reserve price* - Minimum sale price at auction (if known)
- *Auction date* - Date of the proposed auction
- *Agent's remuneration* - The agreed fee including GST, and an example of that fee as the specific sale price
- *Inspection* - Property inspection times and circumstances as agreed
- *Promotional activities* - How the property will be advertised or promoted

- *For sale sign* - Permission to install a signboard
- *Expenses* - Marketing expenses incurred by the agent to be reimbursed by the seller
- *Variation of fees and expenses* - As agreed in writing
- *Deposit* - Agent to hold the deposit in trust
- *Authority to deduct* - Agent to deduct monies as required from deposit on settlement
- *Payment to principal* - Money will be paid by cheque or EFT to nominated account
- *Taxes or deductions* - Agent is entitled to reimbursement if paid on behalf of principal
- *Contract of sale* - Agent must have a copy of the contract available for inspection by prospective buyers
- *Conjunction* - One fee payable if Agent is working in conjunction with another agent
- *Limit of agent's services* - Agent's services in relation to the sale
- *Good and services tax (GST)* - Payable by the Principal to the Agent at the completion date of the sale
- *Agent's indemnity and liability* - In the course of performance of Agent under this agreement
- *Financial and investment advice* - General disclaimer
- *Material fact* - Disclosure as required under the *Property, Stock and Business Agents Act 2002*

- *Privacy policy* - In relation to how the Agent collects, uses and discloses personal information
- *Disclosure* - The Agent discloses any rebates, discounts, commissions or benefits from third parties
- *Principal's authority* - Stating that the Principal is authorised to sign this agreement
- *Acknowledgements* - Relating to the document and its clauses
- *Work, health and safety* - Two clauses in relation to management of the sale
- *Consumer's guide* - Acknowledgement that the Principal has received a copy of the Fair Trading consumer's guide
- *Cooling off period* - In relation to this agreement
- *Signatures* - Of all Principals or Powers of Attorney with date of agreement and Agent's signature.

Importantly, the agency sales agreement is a binding legal document and needs to be considered and treated as such and signed by the authorised parties. If you are unsure of the terms of the agreement, you should seek legal advice. By signing the agency sales agreement you are hiring that agent to sell for you.

If you'd like to request a copy of our agency agreement, please email me at geoff@rwm.com.au .

STEP 4 – THE AGENT'S ESTIMATE OF SELLING PRICE

When an agent lists a property for sale in New South Wales, *The Property, Stock and Business Agents Act 2002* requires that the agent advise the vendor of their estimate of selling price. This is required when completing the agency sales agreement, and best practice is that the agent provides the seller with a written estimate of selling price that complies with the NSW Fair Trading current guidelines. For this reason, as part of our compliance checks, we always provide a written agent's estimate, which is discussed with the seller and signed off by both the seller and the agent as a compliance document for our files. The agent must provide substantiated evidence of their estimate of selling price, not simply choose a figure they think the vendor wants to hear.

Our document includes both descriptive and economic factors to substantiate our estimate:

1. Address of the property to be sold
2. Property features such as condition, location and size of land
3. Main features - providing a brief description of any features that are relevant to the value of the property
4. Recent sales - a list of up to six recent sales that are relevant to establishing the likely selling price. The sales will not be older than six months and we include the address, sale price, date sold and relevant comments

5. Market demand - indicating if the current buyer activity is strong, average or weak
6. Properties for sale - up to six currently listed properties which prospective buyers may consider relevant to our subject property
7. The total number of properties for sale in the subject's suburb and in a specific price range which may be considered competitive to the subject property
8. Existing market conditions - determining if the current market is one of the following:
    - Seller's market - where there are more buyers than sellers
    - Buyer's market - where there are more sellers than buyers
    - Balanced market - where there are equal numbers of buyers and sellers
9. Seasonal factors which may affect the number of listings on the market, such as the time of year, weather patterns, school terms, holiday periods, timing of other events
10. Economic factors such as interest rate variances; the state of the economy; and newsworthy factors that may encourage or discourage buyers from making a purchase, such as interest rate instability, the Royal Commission into banking, an announcement of state or

federal elections, or press or media coverage which is overly sensational

11. Seller information - the instructions or expectations that the seller has expressed, including specific instructions regarding the method of sale and marketing that differ from advice provided by the agent
12. Preferred method of sale - auction, private treaty or expressions of interest
13. Specific instructions - from the seller regarding marketing and expectations
14. Other relevant information considered in estimating the sale price, including restrictions on the use of the land, possible future use of the land (such as zoning, rights of way, resumption, preservation orders, restrictions of use, redevelopment, covenants, or heritage orders)
15. Other items that have been discussed that may impact a buyer's perception of value
16. Conclusion - based on all the information provided in this document, the agent's estimate of the likely selling price for the subject property, defined as \$x - \$y on a specific date.

The seller and the agent co-sign this document, which provides a record of the discussions we have had at the signed date.

It is important to recognise that this is a living document and it is likely that during the campaign any or all of these factors may change, which will in turn affect the estimated sale price.

We are always told that no two properties are alike, so if we are using the comparable sale method to establish an estimate of value, what are the features of the property that affect value?

The long answer is, almost everything, and the short answer is, just look at the big picture.

Agents provide an estimate of value with a price range of 10%, which on a $1 million property could be written as $950,000 - $1,045,000. This range takes in a raft of features and benefits that could be individually itemised to create an extensive list of points of difference for every single property. However, we rarely do this. Our perception of value is not just a list of features and benefits but also includes emotional value: how the property feels to us. Only the buyer can value their feelings and decide if the property they wish to buy is the right one for them. Often, after purchasing a home, they may lament that they probably paid too much but add that they are very happy with their purchase. This expression of buyer's remorse is common, and not the end of the world. Paying too little is a worse outcome, as you never secure the property. An auction is a great example of this: the bidding may get down to the last hundreds of dollars and one buyer may secure the home over the other buyer for perhaps $100. The buyer who offered too little is back on the Saturday inspection merry-go-round, comparing every new property with the one they just missed out on. In many cases, to avoid missing out again, this type of buyer 'pays too much' for the next property and is happy to do so. Emotion plays a huge part in determining value.

It may be necessary to review the estimated value following buyer feedback and new sales activity. The agent's opinion of value in the agency sales agreement may then require variation.

We also complete an identity check form, to ensure that you are the rightful owner of the property and are entitled to sell it. In much the same way as you need 100 points to open a bank account, I need to sight documents such as your passport, driver's licence, Medicare card and documents that tie you to the property, such as council notices, water, power or gas notices that have your name and the property address on them.

With all this paperwork out of the way, we can then turn our attention to your property and the pre-sale preparations to maximise your price.

3. THE PAPERWORK

STEP 1 – YOUR CONVEYANCER

When you signed the agency sales agreement with me, you nominated your conveyancer - and they are an important part of your property team. Along with your real estate agent, your conveyancer is responsible for your sale and how it finally comes together. The conveyancer you appoint works for you. It is their role to represent you throughout the sale, from creation of the contract of sale to the exchange of contracts, through to settlement of the title of the property.

The difference between a lawyer and a conveyancer from a real estate agent's perspective is that a conveyancer specialises in the legal aspects of buying and selling a property (called conveyancing). They do not practise other areas of the law such as family law, corporations law or estate matters. They are property law specialists.

Your conveyancer will be in contact with you to confirm details and they will prepare the legal documents that are required for the real estate transaction. This is essentially the contract of sale. Sellers will be asked to complete a 'vendor's statement' relevant to disclosure laws, and the conveyancer will conduct title and planning searches and attach any ancillary documents needed for the settlement process.

It can take several days to create a contract of sale, depending on waiting times for documentation. Importantly, your real estate agent cannot discuss your property with any potential buyer, or market or advertise the property in any manner, until they have received the contract of sale. This is the law. Agents are not permitted to 'just show a few buyers through your home' without an agency sales agreement and a contract of sale: if they do, severe penalties can apply.

STEP 2 – THE CONTRACT OF SALE

The contract of sale is a legally binding document prepared by the seller's conveyancer to permit the sale and purchase of a property. A real estate agent can't buy or sell property without one, so it's important to make sure it is correct. On receipt of your contract of sale, your agent should check it for accuracy and completeness.

The initial pages of the contract include the following details:

- *Vendor's agent* - Your nominated real estate agency, agent and contact details

- *Co-agent* - If applicable
- *Vendor* - Full name of vendor with correct spelling
- *Vendor's conveyancer* - Firm name, address and contact details
- *Date for completion* - Default period is 42 days after the contract date, but this can be varied
- *Land* - Property address
- *Title reference* - Registered title or strata plan and folio identifier
- *Status* - Tick boxes for 'vacant possession' or 'subject to existing tenancies'
- *Improvements* - Tick boxes for house, garage, carport, home unit, car space, storage space, none, other
- *Attached copies* - Documents in the List of Documents as marked or as numbered, Other Documents.

Then there is a box containing the following items, which a real estate agent is permitted to fill out upon the sale of residential property:

- *Inclusions* - Tick boxes for blinds, built-in wardrobes, clothesline, curtains, dishwasher, fixed floor coverings, insect screens, light fittings, rangehood, solar panels, stove, pool equipment, TV antenna, other (such as wired-in smoke detectors, remote controls, air conditioners, garden pots)

- *Exclusions* - Anything that is not included with the sale
- *Purchaser* - Full name(s) of all purchasers
- *Purchaser's conveyancer* - Full contact details
- *Price* - Agreed sale price
- *Deposit* - 10% of the price unless otherwise stated
- *Balance* - Remaining to be paid
- *Contract date*

The remaining part of the contract is outside the box that real estate agents are permitted to complete, and contains the following details:

- *Buyers agent* - If applicable
- *Vendor's signature*
- *Witness's signature* for vendor
- *Purchaser's signature*
- *Witness's signature* for purchaser
- *Purchaser* - Tick boxes for 'Joint Tenants', 'Tenants in Common' and 'In Unequal Shares'
- The vendor then has the following tick boxes to choose from:
  - Deposit bond acceptance
  - Proposed electronic transaction (standard from 1 July 2019)

  - Land tax is adjustable/not adjustable
  - GST is a taxable supply/not a taxable supply
  - Margin scheme will be used in making the taxable supply and details of the sale not being a taxable supply
  - Purchaser to make a Residential Withholding Payment, further details relating to payment
- *Checklist of included documents*
- *Holder of strata or community title records*
  - If applicable.

The contract of sale then has two notices to Sellers and Buyers. The first is to do with smoke or heat alarms required under the *Environmental Planning and Assessment Act 1979*. The second is to do with loose-fill asbestos, often referred to as 'loose-fill asbestos insulation', which in New South Wales prior to 1985 was pumped into roof areas of residential properties, by companies like Mr Fluffy. This does not refer to asbestos sheeting that may have been used in the construction of garages or eaves.

The contract then contains a page relating to the cooling off period, specifically the purchaser's rights to rescind a contract or whether the buyer's conveyancer has provided a 66W waiver of the cooling off period to make the exchange of contract unconditional.

It then includes a page of warnings relating to various Acts of Parliament and other matters which may affect the rights of those involved with this contract. This includes leases, money owed, transfers, insurance, stamp duty, release of the deposit, personal property, finance, GST and foreign resident capital gains withholding tax, even if the seller is not a foreign resident.

The contract then provides some 14 pages containing some 31 clauses and subclauses which make up the basis of the contract and the provisions under which the property is bought and sold. Following these clauses, the seller's conveyancer may choose to include additional conditions annexed as clauses specific to their contract of sale.

I find that many sellers have little interest in the contract at the start of a sale, but should something go wrong - and it sometimes does - they rush to see what the contract says when it may be too late to change it.

Disclaimer: I am not a lawyer/solicitor or conveyancer and cannot and do not offer any legal advice of any kind whatsoever. All interested parties should make their own enquiries and undertake their own due diligence.

STEP 3 – DOCUMENTS RELATING TO THE CONTRACT OF SALE

As well as the standard clauses in the contract of sale, in New South Wales additional documents are required to be included if applicable. These include a swimming pool compliance, Foreign Investment Review Board certification and a tax clearance certificate. While not mandatory, a property land survey is also always helpful in establishing boundaries.

Additionally, as your agent, I need to know about any recent improvements to your property, so I will ask you for supporting documentation regarding the following:

- Cost and/or receipts of any recent property improvements and what was done
- Property survey (if available)
- Property valuation (must be less than six months old)
- Pre-sale builder's inspection
- Occupation certificate from council
- Builder's warranty receipt
- Transferable guarantees relating to items like swimming pool equipment or air conditioners
- Original or historical documents or past sales information about the home
- Alarm or security company details and codes
- Contact details for tradespeople who are familiar with the home, gardeners, cleaners, and maintenance people
- Development application or any approved plans
- Current utility receipts for water, gas, electricity, council or strata fees
- Keys for access to all doors, including garage, laundry or storage areas.

I'll also ask for information on solar power, watering systems, water tanks, parking arrangements, garbage collection nights, building manager details and anything else that I should know which could be considered a 'material fact' and which may influence the buyer's decision to purchase the property.

STEP 4 – INCLUSIONS AND EXCLUSIONS

The contract of sale front-page box allows a real estate agent to put a cross in the box of the preassigned inclusions and hand-write in any *other* inclusions and any exclusions. The reason for this is that in most cases, while the conveyancer has prepared the contract of sale and requested information from the seller in relation to inclusions and exclusions, they may not have inspected the property so may be unable to determine what is actually in the property or not.

The standard boxed inclusions are blinds, built-in wardrobes, clothesline, curtains, dishwasher, fixed floor coverings, insect screens, light fittings, rangehood, solar panels, stove, pool equipment, TV antenna and 'other'.

An inclusion is generally considered to be anything that is fixed to the property, hence the use of terminology like 'built-in' wardrobes and 'fixed floor' coverings. It does not include furnishings such as free-standing wardrobes or anything that can readily be picked up and moved.

STEP 5 – FAIR TRADING COMPLIANCE

There was always honour in shaking hands. In the old days 'a deal is a deal' was the order of the day. However, it's no longer possible to do business the old-fashioned way.

NSW Fair Trading is the government body that real estate agents answer to in New South Wales. (For a list of comparable government bodies in each state and territory see page 175.) As a seller, when you sign your sales agency agreement you acknowledge receipt of the consumer guide *Agency Agreements for the Sale of Residential Property* from the agent prior to signing the agreement.

There are two 'fact sheets' released by Fair Trading in conjunction with the Real Estate Institute of NSW (REINSW) which we often provide at our open homes to assist purchasers with making an offer and bidding at auctions. You can find these fact sheets at www.fairtrading.nsw.gov.au and www.reinsw.com.au.

NSW Fair Trading oversees and administers the conduct of real estate agents in relation to the *Property, Stock and Business Agents Act 2002* and the Property, Stock and Business Agents Regulation 2014 and the Australian Consumer Law. The industry is always under review for ongoing improvements to assist property owners, purchasers and real estate agents when buying and selling property. As such, the laws are always evolving and licensed real estate agents and auctioneers like myself are constantly attending training sessions to stay up to date - and of course we are required to engage in annual continuous personal development courses as part of maintaining our licence and credentials.

Consequently, many of our checklists and processes are in place to ensure compliance with the law and to ensure we are transparent and accountable in all our business dealings. I am obligated to act in my clients' best interests at all times, and compliance documents help me to deliver the most rewarding real estate experience for you. Make sure the real estate agent you work with is up to date with all compliance requirements.

4. PREPARATION

STEP 1 – HOUSE OF HORRORS

The saying is true in real estate: you only get one chance to make a first impression. Many times, when I'm asked to inspect a property, the owners say 'Oh, it's a bit of a mess, but you'll see past that' - and they are not kidding.

I have sold all types of properties in all types of conditions.

I have sold houses for hoarders: that is, where the occupant literally keeps everything because in their mind everything has an actual value and should be kept. Newspapers are piled up to head height, so there is literally just one thin track to allow you to navigate between rooms, with some rooms not accessible at all.

I have sold homes with so much mould growing on the walls and ceilings that it was difficult to breathe, and the occupant was telling me that for some unknown reason they have a nagging cough that won't go away, and you could literally see the mould spores floating in the air.

I have even sold a home in which one bedroom was a dedicated indoor aviary with fifty birds living in the room. That same house had pigeons that flew from room to room and the owner's instructions were to put my hands on my head to stop the pigeons from landing in my hair.

I have sold properties with fist holes in the walls or doors from domestic violence. It's always shocking to see and is a reminder that in any suburb there may be problems behind closed doors that we are not aware of.

I have sold many deceased estates which are almost unliveable. It's quite a shock to see.

I have sold properties where the owner has just up and left without paying the bank. The Sheriff has taken possession, changed the locks and put up 'Do Not Enter' signage. I have been contacted by the bank to sell the property to recover their loan, so the sale is 'mortgagee-in-possession'.

When I am asked to sell an estate property which still has all the past owner's belongings inside, I never know what I might find. Over the years, I have found historical documents and photographs that were passed on to the local library, valuable paintings that were sent off to be auctioned, personal items such as watches, rings and pendants, and once a large sum of cash stashed in a biscuit tin at the back of the pantry.

I have sold a house with no floors - they had literally rotted away. The roof was damaged, so the rain just poured in and broke through the plaster ceiling, and the water rotted the timber floorboards until the whole floor collapsed. It wasn't safe for home inspections. I had to put up an orange construction roll-out fence and signage to stop buyers from entering. They could look from the doorway and circle the house to look in through the windows, but they could not enter the house as it just wasn't safe. Some homes I have sold were without doubt in the 'renovate or detonate' category.

Thanks to all those prime-time TV renovation shows, everyone fancies themselves as an owner-builder. Therefore, the interest in a property that needs a complete makeover is often surprisingly high - it often sells for far more than you expect, simply because buyers get carried away with the idea of 'renovating to flip' with a big payday on resale.

Many times, buyers underestimate the cost of renovations and are disappointed to hear that their finished home is worth less than they spent on it. Then I find out that the reason for selling is that their relationship has turned sour during the stress of the build.

Real estate agents meet people at both ends of the emotional spectrum. It's not always easy to manage both sides of a deteriorating relationship and juggle the demands of buyers with the expectations of the sellers, particularly when the sellers may not even be talking to one another.

Pre-sale can be a challenging time and I am pretty sure over all these years that I have worked on every challenging situation you can think of. For the most part, pre-sale preparations can be handled by the owner with some guidance from myself or one of my trusted professionals who specialise in decluttering and other pre-sale preparation, providing both physical and emotional support during a difficult time.

STEP 2 – YOUR SET-TO-SELL SCORE

Life is messy. We live our lives a little bit at home, a little bit at work, some of it at school or university, hopefully some of it on holidays and often too much of it in our car or on the bus or train. So we are not focused on home maintenance and making sure our house is well maintained.

As project managers, we have developed a simple tool to help you know if your property is sale-ready. It's called your 'set-to-sell scorecard'. It's something we invented to help sellers take stock of their home. It's unique to us and helps you to know if your property is sale-ready. Your set-to-sell score is out of a maximum of 100 points and tells us if you are ready to sell now.

Most homes are not ready to sell the day the sellers decide they'd like to sell. Most people need some help understanding which maintenance items or tasks will add value to their final sale price and which will not.

What do we cover?

Our set-to-sell scorecard assesses your property with a score out of 10 on the following 10 criteria:

1. Curb appeal
2. Declutter
3. Cleanliness

4. Painting/grout/silicone
5. Easily forgotten repairs
6. Lighting
7. Presentation
8. Storage
9. Head space
10. Senses

When rating your property, we will walk through from the front gate to the back fence and give you a score based on your current look and feel of the place. We will then provide you with simple tips on how to improve your score in the most cost-effective way, so you have the very best chance of selling for top dollar in a reasonable timeframe and you also enjoy a rewarding and profitable real estate experience.

Importantly, when your home is on the market, it is competing with all the other homes on the market at the same time - you are never on the market alone. Your set-to-sell score is a benchmark for how buyers will perceive your property against other homes they are inspecting. Homes that look and feel loved will sell for more money faster than homes that have room for some improvement.

STEP 3 – SYSTEMS AND CHECKLISTS

I love systems and checklists. They save me time doing repetitive tasks and they keep me on track, so I don't miss anything. Experienced pilots still run through their checklists before every single flight to ensure everything will be as they expect it will be. 'No surprises' is a good way to fly and it's the same with my real estate business.

One of the biggest complaints about agents is that they don't communicate enough with their clients, so their clients don't feel that they are in control of the sales process when they should be. I have sold many properties for clients I've never even met. It doesn't matter where my clients are located, because my systems and processes provide accountability and transparency. For instance, I have an online system that provides you with a portal password so that you can log in 24/7 and see exactly where we are in the sale process and what we have accomplished together so far. I am always looking for new and better ways of refining the sales experience to ensure that your real estate experience with me is the best it can be.

Ask the agent you are talking to about their systems and checklists.

STEP 4 – RENTAL APPRAISAL

We invite our leasing manager to inspect homes we are selling and prepare a letter that includes an estimated rental return. This is on display at our open homes to give buyers, and particularly investors, an accurate rental figure, so they can do their numbers if they are purchasing the property to rent out. This adds certainty and allows buyers to make an informed decision and move quickly from being interested to being ready to make an offer.

If the property is a rental property and the tenants are still in residence, then their lease agreement is included as part of the contract of sale, and it clearly states what the tenants are paying per calendar month. If the tenant has recently moved out, and perhaps that is the trigger for the owner to want to sell, then we assess the property using the last paid rent as a guide. We also assess the current market to determine the future rent, as it may have increased or decreased since the tenants originally moved in.

STEP 5 – SELLING A VACANT PROPERTY

One of the advantages of selling any property while it is vacant is that your agent has 24/7 access to show the home at any time. In addition to your agent's scheduled open homes, they can market and advertise the property as 'inspect by appointment with agent' to show it anytime.

In most cases, styling the home (more about this in chapter 5) is a better option than selling it unfurnished. Your investment in styling will attract more buyers in a shorter time and will add up to a better selling experience and a higher sale price for you. Furnishing the home will change the focus of buyers, from looking at the original state of the home to imagining themselves moving into the home.

At a bare minimum, your agent should be visiting and checking on the property at least once a week. During these visits, they will:

- Check the signboard is still correctly positioned
- Check no one has been inside as an unauthorised guest

- Check that the gardener has been mowing the lawn and doing the garden on schedule
- Check that the electricity is still connected and your timer lights are still active
- Check for any strange smells in or around the house - particularly dead rodents
- Check for dead bugs lying around, and sweep or vacuum the floors
- Flush the toilets and check that the taps are not leaking
- Check the garage door is closed and that the house is locked and secure
- Check and empty the letterbox, and collect the local paper and advertising flyers
- Make a note of anything that should be brought to the owner's attention and have it attended to.

STEP 6 – PROPERTY INFORMATION SHEET

We create a comprehensive buyer's information sheet for every property we sell. We know what questions buyers are going to ask, so we try and answer them all in detail on this sheet.

The information we provide for a house will include the following items:

- Property address
- Number of bedrooms, bathrooms and garages, and any interesting features

- Our estimated price range
- Our agents' names, phone numbers and email addresses
- The land size of the property, taken from the contract survey or a reliable source such as RP Data
- Water rates
- Council rates
- Parking
- Current or potential development subject to council approval
- Rental estimate if the buyer may be planning to lease the home
- Description of the property with bullet-point features
- Local area sales within the last six months which are relevant to this property
- Disclaimer.

Additional information for strata properties (flats, apartments or condominiums) includes:

- The strata plan number and lot number
- The registered strata date, which is a guide to the age of the building
- Total size on title and, where possible, internal size, balcony size, carpark size and storage size
- Quarterly strata and sinking levies
- Administration and capital works fund totals at the time of the report

- Strata manager's contact details
- Number of units in the building
- Parking, additional notes
- Pets - whether there is a by-law or pets are considered on individual application
- Laundry details - shared facilities for washer and dryer; owner-supplied; or strata-managed coin-operated machines
- Clotheslines, if available, and their location
- Storage, either general storage room or individual storage cages allocated to each unit
- Rental estimate based on other current rentals in the building
- Ratio of owner-occupiers to tenants in the building
- A note that a strata report is available on request at no charge
- Property and location description
- Local area sales, including most recent sold property in the building.

Essentially, we are answering every question a buyer may have before they ask us. At the end of a long day of inspections, the buyer may have seen four or five properties and our buyer's information sheet provides them with all the 'fast facts' they need to know to help them make a decision more quickly.

5. GETTING SALE READY

STEP 1 – STYLING

To style or not to style? That is the question.

I sell a range of apartments and houses of all shapes and sizes. The only rule that I follow is to make whatever is the best decision for the seller. The property will certainly look more attractive if the seller hires a stylist, but it's the owner's choice and I respect that.

When the seller is willing to update and style but simply doesn't have the ready cash to do it, there are now finance options for home preparations and styling. These are effectively no-interest loans specifically for selling your home. Obviously, terms and conditions apply; however, if you meet the criteria, this may be a good option to maximise your presentation for sale. Ask your agent for details.

The main costs for styling a home are the transport costs: the physical moving of furniture and items from the warehouse to your property and back again. Leaving the furniture in your property for an extended period is the negotiable part.

If you are not prepared to style the property, you have several other options; let's look each of these in turn.

Leave the property empty

You can empty the property altogether and opt for the blank canvas look. This is often the best-case scenario with a deceased estate property that may be very run down. If the property needs to be knocked down or extensively renovated before it can be lived in, then styling it will not help sell it. It will look awkward with new furniture in an original condition room.

Use what you have

This is often the best decision when the rooms in a property are fairly original and the existing furniture is what you would expect to see in a home of that era. Often all you really need to do is a good clean, and then remove all but the basic pieces of furniture, replace the lightbulbs with brighter bulbs, pull back the curtains, open the blinds and buy lots of fresh flowers. At least buyers won't mistake it for another styled property they saw that day.

Mix it up

Some stylists will use a mixture of your existing furniture and some extra pieces they bring in. It's half style and half your own. Bear in mind, though, that most stylists have a minimum charge which may not make this a viable option.

Virtual styling

Virtual furniture is an option for a property which is vacant, but where the budget is not available to hire furniture and have it moved in and leased for weeks at a time for an ongoing fee. Instead, the property is photographed empty and then computer images of furniture are placed in the room, to create a finished photo that can be used online to make the property look more attractive than just empty rooms. Virtual furnished photographs carry a disclaimer that they are in fact virtually furnished, but done properly this allows you to market the property looking its best - although the illusion is quickly diminished when a buyer walks through the door into an empty room.

STEP 2 – TIMING

'When do you want to be sold by?' and 'Why?' are very important questions.

Another way of looking at the timing is by asking 'What date would you like the auction to be?' so that we have a date to work towards. There is no guarantee that your property will be sold by auction day, but you and your agent need a common goal. Once the auction date is agreed, you can work backwards and see how much time you have to put everything in place. Often you have less time than you imagined, especially when you are thinking of bringing in tradies such as painters or floor polishers to make your house ship-shape.

We create a calendar with you to visualise the preparations, with dates attached to ensure we are working on a realistic timeframe. The calendar is colour-coded so we can see at a glance what activities are planned and when they will occur.

Once the property preparations are done, we adjust the calendar to show the timeline from styling or final home preparations to photography; creation of the floorplan and writing of the selling copy; owner's approval of the marketing elements including approval of the brochure; signboard and website, prior to printing brochures and launching the property online.

There are external forces at play here that can affect the timeline, such as public holidays, school holidays, the Easter break and the Christmas break. We need to consider school holidays in the context of a house where the target market is a family looking for a family home. Even though the family buyer's priority may be to purchase a home, they also make travel arrangements in school holidays, so many will simply be out of town or out of the country if we launch a property at the start of the holidays.

Auction campaigns usually involve four weeks of scheduled opens - that is, a mid-week and a Saturday open - but depending on where school holidays and public holidays fall, we can extend the campaign to five weeks or shorten it to three weeks as necessary.

Each year, property sales peak in February or March following the Christmas break, when buyers and sellers are motivated to start the year with a success. The other busy months are October and November, when buyers want to secure a property before Christmas. The rest of the year is consistent. Winter is the perfect time to sell apartments or homes without yards and gardens, but many large homes look and feel better in spring. The best time to sell is when you are ready. I have clients who sit down with me to plan their sale in six months' time, to have time to do what needs to be done to be on the market at the right time for them.

STEP 3 – VENDOR PAID MARKETING

Vendor paid marketing is when the owner of the property takes responsibility for the promotion of their own property, but is working with their real estate agent to ensure that no stone is left unturned in the hunt for the ideal buyer for their home.

This is the point of realisation that selling is a collaborative effort and that to be a team player the seller needs to have skin in the game. The saying is, 'You can't sell a secret', and the reality is that is mostly the case. Although we do sell properties off market without advertising, most properties are taken to market in the traditional way.

As your agent, I have every marketing option available to promote your home. Together we choose the most effective marketing strategy, and custom-design our campaign to reach the most buyers. Although we want our marketing to have 'reach', it must be targeted reach, so that the property is exposed to potential buyers, not just everyone who may like it but is not looking to buy it.

We know that almost all active buyers will first look for a property on the internet. They may also drive down a street and see a signboard. Or they may see a home advertised in the paper while at the coffee shop. That's why we use a mix of different marketing platforms to find your ideal buyer.

It's often the combination of marketing elements that allows your ideal buyer to find your property. It's not one single promotion in isolation, but all the elements put together that creates the perfect storm.

Ideally, to leave no stone unturned you would choose every possible marketing option to sell your home. However, the cost would be considerable and there are no guarantees.

Many sellers work to a budget, rather than choosing the combinations of elements that will give them the largest reach to the most targeted groups. Can you remember where you saw your home advertised before you bought it? Our goal is to find a buyer for your house who is, in many ways, just like you, so where should we advertise your home to find someone like you? The answer will most likely be, multiple places.

STEP 4 – BOOK THE AUCTIONEER

Not all property is sold at auction, so this step in the process may not be relevant to you. However, for those readers considering selling at auction, it is vital to understand this step.

Every great auction needs a great auctioneer and we work with some of the best in the business. Saturday is the busiest day for auctions and most auctions are held on site, at the property, because it helps build emotion. Nothing beats the auctioneer pointing to a view and asking the crowd, 'What's that view worth?' and having them all look at the view and want to own it. That's raw emotion and that's what an auction is all about - delivering the very best price from the emotional buyers gathered in one place on auction day.

The auctioneer plays a crucial part in the process, so we need to be sure that the auctioneer we want is available to work for us at the time and on the day that we want them.

We book our auctioneer for a one-hour slot several weeks in advance. Just like booking a hotel room, you need to confirm payment. Whether you arrive and stay the night or not. you will be charged for that room. Whether the auctioneer is needed on the day or not, we are paying for their time. If the property is negotiated and sold the week before auction, we still have our auctioneer booked and they can't reasonably expect to find another auction to fill our our last-minute cancellation, so we pay for their time whether we take advantage of it or not.

The right auctioneer will pull together all your agent's hard work over the past four weeks to deliver a great result for you. Sometimes, my clients have told me after a successful auction that the auctioneer was actually a magician in disguise - they can literally pull a rabbit out of a hat to get the sale result that puts a smile across your face.

On the other hand, if on auction day there are no registered bidders, the auctioneer is still on site to manage the auction process, so we pay for their services. The auctioneer is a non-refundable investment in the success of your sale.

STEP 5 – PEST AND BUILDING REPORT

I ask our sellers to invest in an independent building and pest inspection report and make it available to potential buyers at no charge. This serves two purposes. Firstly, it helps sellers to understand if there are any problems with their home and, if there are, we have an opportunity to repair those items that raised an eyebrow. We can undertake repair and maintenance items before marketing the home and then have the building inspector reinspect the property and adjust the report accordingly.

This saves a lot of frustration when a buyer negotiates to put an unrealistic repair cost on an item which could have been repaired before marketing. An up-to-date termite and pest report with a clean bill of health will give the buyer greater confidence to make an offer and move forward.

Some building inspection companies require the buyer to pay for part or for all of the building report, so that a transferable insurance policy covers them for any omission by the inspector. When we supply the report at no charge to buyers, we are not offering any insurance and they are aware of that.

Additionally, if a building inspection has been completed on a property, the law states that the agent must advise all buyers and provide the building inspector's details to all buyers in case they wish to contact the inspector to purchase the same report. However, the building inspector is not obliged to either sell them the report or lower his fee for additional copies.

STEP 6 – STRATA REPORT

When a buyer is interested in buying a property, they will request a contract of sale. When they are serious about buying, they will forward that contract of sale to their conveyancer. The first thing the conveyancer will ask for is a copy of the pest and building report for a house or the strata report for an apartment. We know they will ask for these reports, so it makes sense to have them done so we can provide them immediately, without delay.

Whenever we are selling a strata property, we ask the vendor to pay for an independent strata report compiled by a third-party inspector. Buyers rarely require a building inspection for a strata property, as the building is maintained by the committee and the strata manager, and the details of their maintenance plan and expenditure are included in the strata report.

If the agent does not supply a strata report, then each individual buyer needs to arrange, through their conveyancer, to have a third party make an appointment at the strata manager's office to view the file and meeting minutes and compile their own version of a strata report for their own use. This may take several days, and the buyer may lose interest. In my experience, time kills deals.

Different companies will provide similar information in different formats, but essentially a strata report is compiled from the information held at the strata manager's office. This information may or may not be complete, so check the strata report for these details:

- Strata plan number, lot number, address and inspection date
- Disclaimer
- Strata roll/records
- Mortgages
- Entitlement
- Building insurance
- Public liability insurance
- Voluntary workers insurance
- Other insurances
- Broker details
- Last property valuation date and value
- Levies
- Last levy increase/decrease
- Special levies
- Proposed special levies
- Books of account with balance of the administrative fund and capital works fund
- Maintenance levies/expenses

- Finance and loans
- By-laws - any recent changes, any exclusive use, any pet references?
- Managing agent's details
- Notices and orders, approvals and consent
- Title deed
- General information regarding lots, titles, unit of entitlement, aggregate unit of entitlement
- Fire safety statement
- Asbestos report
- History of disputes
- Building matters
- Pest control
- Window safety compliance certificate
- Statement of financial position
- Statement of financial performance
- Owner's ledger
- Certificate of currency for insurances
- Proposed budget
- Annual fire and electrical statement
- Sinking fund forecast
- Minutes of annual general meetings
- Attachments

Minutes of meetings will vary but may include:

- Persons present or by proxy
- Minutes of previous meetings
- Motions
- Manner of voting
- Financial statements
- Auditor's report
- Capital works fund balance
- Work health and safety
- Asbestos report and register
- Termite inspection
- Fire safety
- Levy due dates
- Sinking fund plan
- Budget and levy
- Levy amounts
- Insurance
- Valuation
- Committee candidates
- Office bearers and appointments
- Committee limitations
- Committee delegation
- General business

- Supplier reviews
- Service of notices
- Management reports
- By-law notices
- By-law review
- Building or grounds repairs and maintenance
- Quotes
- Arrears collection
- Works application
- Unauthorised renovation - updates and notices
- Close of meeting.

If a strata report is not available and the buyer does not intend to pay to arrange one, many conveyancers will ask the buyer to sign a statement saying that they have chosen not to arrange a strata report. Providing the strata report builds trust between the agent and the buyer and speeds up offers leading to a sale.

STEP 7 – KEYS, REMOTES AND PETS

As your agent, to show your home effectively I need to know how things work around your house. You need to share a few home secrets with me. I need a full set of keys. I need access to anywhere that a buyer may reasonably ask to inspect that will affect the price they pay for the property.

I like to get a rundown from the owner on who their neighbours are. Buyers often ask about the neighbours and it builds trust to be able to give them the correct information. In a strata building, buyers like to know the ratio of owner-occupiers to tenants so they have some understanding of the make-up of their potential neighbours.

For open inspections, it's always best if dogs or cats can leave the property with the owners before each inspection. Not all buyers are pet lovers, and litter trays or dog poos in the garden can be a turn-off. Yes, it has happened that a potential buyer has walked dog poo unknowingly back into the house and across the carpet, before realising and either announcing it to everyone present or saying nothing at all. Unfortunately, the open house is never the same after that moment.

Not all buildings allow pets, so your agent needs to know if there are any pets living in your strata building now and what the owners' corporation policy is on keeping pets.

STEP 8 – PROFESSIONAL PHOTOGRAPHY

Your agent will arrange for a professional photographer to photograph your property to present its very best features. Not every property will look like it belongs in a designer home magazine, and that's OK: we will do the very best with what we have. Sometimes, through circumstance, that means the property is presented vacant or includes tenants' belongings, or it is offered as an estate property.

The secret of professional photography is balance. Getting the balance of what is included in the photo and what is left out is an art form, and it makes all the difference to how your property presents. Consequently, when photographing your property, the photographer will likely move things around to achieve the most pleasing photos. This may mean moving tables, chairs, buffets, lamps, lounges - in fact anything and everything. You will be amazed at the difference between creating photographs and just taking photographs.

In addition to still photography, you may choose to have a video produced. The video crew will shoot moving images that showcase your home to create a one- or two-minute movie set to music and with a voice-over. You can also choose aerial drone still images or video images to show your property's location, views or special amenities. Drones are nimble enough now to shoot video from above your house and then fly through an open door into the house all in one shot. A video of your home can be a combination of still images and moving pictures which highlight your favourite features.

Buyers are expecting to see professional photos, and property styling and professional photography go hand in hand. It can be a challenge when a property has a tenant living there during the campaign, but the agent needs to take control and outline their expectations in such a way that the tenants always keep the property 'photo ready'.

Never underestimate the power of professional photography to attract buyers to your home.

STEP 9 – FLOORPLAN AND SITE PLAN

The floorplan is an essential marketing tool, because it allows buyers to understand the flow of the property to be able to decide if it works for them.

The floorplan is a scaled drawing of the property as seen from overhead. It allows buyers to understand the relationship between rooms and the overall layout of the property. The floorplan also helps buyers with a summary of the property at a glance. Importantly, they can see the size of rooms, as the dimensions are given on the floorplan. They can also see if all the bedrooms have built-in robes or just some of them.

The floorplan shows windows and doors, which gives an idea of how light the rooms are and how private. Balconies or outdoor areas are shown on the floorplan, plus any parking and storage areas. It also has a compass point showing north.

There are many types of floorplans now, including 2D and 3D versions, many with furnishings to show that a bedroom has a bed in it. Buyers tell me, however, that they prefer a clean floorplan and a pen to allow them to draw their furniture in themselves.

The floorplan for a house should also include a site plan that shows where the house sits in relation to the land size, and any improvements such as a swimming pool, verandah, decks, the driveway and garage. A site plan helps buyers understand the use of the block of land and what part of the land may be available for additions, extensions or parking.

STEP 10 – COPY

'Tell me about your home: why have you loved living here?' This is an important question to ask all owner-occupiers to get a feel for the home and why it has been a part of their life. The question is designed to evoke emotion, because emotion sells homes and buyers purchase homes for lifestyle.

Anyone can write a list of features of a home, but only a copywriter is skilled in choosing the right words that create emotion for the reader to trigger that desire to inspect, which will lead to a compelling feeling in that buyer to purchase and own that home.

We ask owners to put things in their own words to tell us what they love about their home. Your agent can weave these 'gems' into their conversations with buyers to help them connect. Examples of this may be:

- Waking up to the birds in the garden each morning
- Enjoying the level stroll to the coffee shop
- Meeting neighbours along the way
- Taking the dog to the dog park on weekends
- Catching the afternoon sun in the back room
- Enjoying a good book and a glass of wine on a summer's afternoon on the deck.

These are owners' own feelings that the agent will transfer to the buyer through conversation, to move the buyer from a logical viewpoint to an emotional one and encourage them to pay a premium price for the home.

STEP 11 – SIGNBOARD AND BROCHURE

Signboards have come a long way in recent years. These days you have a wide choice. We use a large picture sign with one or more photos of your property, plus bullet points, open times and the auction date, so that anyone passing can't help but get the message. You can go to the next level with a solar illuminated sign if your budget allows, or even install a video sign with your own customised video message on display.

Some sellers don't want a signboard as they don't want to tell the neighbours they are selling. But neighbours buy houses too, and neighbours are advocates of the area as they already live there. Neighbours may also be renting and looking to buy. Neighbours can tell people they know and like about your house, so they get to choose their own new neighbours.

Signboards are rented for the campaign - you don't have to buy them. The suppliers create the sign, deliver and install it safely, monitor and manage it during the campaign and will even assist with maintenance in case of storm damage or graffiti. Then they remove it after the sale and recycle it.

The brochure

The property brochure is essential. It's the 'take-away' that every buyer takes with them and most buyers hang on to. Some end up in the garden, but we keep an eye out for those! The brochure reminds buyers of the home they just saw. The agent presents it after the buyer has provided their details at the front door. Many buyers turn straight to the floorplan and orientate themselves as they walk around. The brochure may have several photos that allow the buyer to show their friends. 'Hey, we inspected this house, what do you think?' It gives them the chance to ask a trusted friend's opinion. It's visual, it's immediate, you can write notes on it and connect with a home.

Of course, brochures are like signboards: as the seller, you have a choice. Many sellers are happy with the double-sided colour paper brochure, while some homeowners may prefer a four-page glossy brochure that says 'This is an expensive house' - the choice is yours. We can even make up a bound booklet with specifications, the property survey and neighbourhood information if you like.

STEP 12 – ON DISPLAY

When buyers inspect a property, they expect the selling agent to be knowledgeable about the property and the area, and their expectations may be very high indeed. They ask questions and expect answers. Open homes are about discovery, so we provide and display as much information at our open homes to answer all the questions from buyers before they even ask them. We know what their questions will be, so we provide the answers and this gives buyers confidence in us.

We hand buyers a property brochure and a Buyer's Information Sheet and we display the following information.

Photos of building amenities

When a strata building has a pool, a gym, a ground floor laundry, a storage cage or even just a car space, most buyers are curious about them. We display a photo of all the amenities on the table in the open home, and on the first inspection most buyers are satisfied they understand what is on offer. This saves a lot of running around.

Strata plan

We highlight the strata plan from the contract, showing the location of the garage and the apartment. We will escort buyers to the facilities on request, but we also minimise those requests by providing the photographs, saving everyone valuable time on open home day.

Full strata report

This report is bound for easy reading and some buyers will always pick it up and flick through it. If they request it, we will email them a copy. The strata report removes a barrier to negotiation by putting both the good and the bad on the table, so buyers can make their own decisions and move forward. Some of the key points buyers are interested to know are the current funds in the building and administration accounts, the harmony of the building, the maintenance costs and any proposed special levies.

Community feature sheet

In the community feature sheet, we include a neighbourhood profile, location details, demographics, public transport travel times, primary and secondary school details, public library location and details of shops and services, parks, fitness and recreation facilities nearby. It's all about making an out-of-area buyer comfortable that the location of this property is just what they are looking for. After all, out-of-area buyers are known to pay a premium price over many locals.

Business cards

We offer a DL-sized card with our details on it and our printed business card available for buyers to put in their pocket. Our alternate business card is also available to take home. This is a microfibre cloth printed with our contact details, ideal for cleaning glasses or any mobile device. More than half the buyers inspecting a property will be wearing glasses and all will have a phone with them, so when they are offered a 'business card you can clean your glasses or phone with' - a smile creeps over their face and they say, 'Yes, I could use one of those'.

Stamp duty guide

Sometimes, as a seller, we forget that in addition to the price that makes us smile, the buyer is required to pay stamp duty. We provide a take-home chart with price points and stamp duty figures as they apply in New South Wales as a ready reference.

Finance broker card

When possible, we invite a trusted finance broker to attend open homes to chat with buyers about the loan process. It pays to get a second opinion on finance, so we display the contact details of our finance partner to assist our buyers.

Rental estimate letter

We display a letter from our property offering their rental estimate. Investors are all about numbers, so we provide the right information for them to do their numbers.

Lastly, we offer complimentary items such as Tim Tam chocolate biscuits, pens and tape measures. Buyers often ask if they can borrow a pen, so it just makes sense to say, 'Please keep that pen with my compliments'. Buyers may also ask how wide the fridge space is or what size the microwave space is, so I keep a supply of small tape measures on hand that they can keep with them while they are inspecting the property.

So many times, buyers have turned to us at open homes and said, 'Thank you, we wish all agents provided the level of service and information that you do'.

STEP 13 – PRIVACY NOTICE

By law, in New South Wales, agents are required to display a privacy notice at the entrance to any property that they are showing as an open home. This notice is required by the Office of Fair Trading to inform buyers that the *Privacy Act 1988* regulates the collection and use, disclosure and maintenance of personal information collected by real estate agents from people attending open for inspections.

It also provides details of where the buyer can view the information collected about them to correct it, update it or ask the information to be removed from the real estate agent's records. We collect names and numbers for security reasons, and to allow the agent to call the buyer after the inspection. This allows us to determine their level of interest and allows them to give feedback to the property owner.

Check the privacy laws in your state or territory via the list of contacts at the back of this book.

STEP 14 – MARKETING APPROVALS

When communication is poor, marketing is one area in which sellers can be disappointed, because they may be expecting something different to what they receive. The design of our marketing fits a format that was created to meet our corporate guidelines, however there are still choices to make to ensure you are happy with the presentation. For instance, we can choose from three background colour styles and between one-, three- or four-photograph designs, plus either text or bullet points. To ensure we get it right, we ask you to proof and confirm all marketing pieces prior to print.

Once the photographs, copy, floorplan, brochure, signboard and flyers are complete, proofed and approved, we have them printed. We also build the property website and post it on our internal web platform so that the seller can check and approve it before we go live on the external sites such as realestate.com.au and domain.com.au.

It's easy to think to yourself, 'I'll just leave all the approvals to the agent', but without a system in place to ensure the proofs are seen by the seller, there is always the chance of a typo or mistake.

6. PROPERTY PRE-LAUNCH

STEP 1 – VIP PREVIEWS

One of the first questions a potential seller asks is 'Do you have any buyers for my home?'

Every agent will answer 'Yes', because every time an agent markets a home, we meet buyers - either new buyers who have just stepped into the market or buyers whom we have met before. An important part of what real estate agents do is to qualify buyers, so we have a good understanding of the type of buyer we are dealing with. These are some of the buyers we meet:

- **HOT buyers** - They have just sold and are keen to buy again as soon as possible, or they have their home on the market and will soon be sold, so again they want to buy as soon as possible.

- **JUST AS HOT buyers** - They have recently sold and may be living with parents or renting another home they don't like, and are ready to buy a home they do like.
- **WARM buyers** - They are doing some research in the area and will try and buy if they find the right property, they are still flexible on their ideal location.
- **COLD buyers** - Neighbours or stickybeaks, not looking to buy. They may be thinking of selling but, if they did, they would likely move out of the area and buy somewhere else.

One of the questions I ask when I meet a buyer at an open home is a very simple one, but it helps to break the ice in a non-confrontational way, so the buyer feels like they can open up to me and start a conversation that helps me to best be able to help them. That question is simply 'Hello - may I ask, are you buying or browsing today?'

Buyers who enquire on a property which is not quite right for them, but who are open to considering other similar properties in the future, are VIP buyers. I may be selling a three-bedroom home in Cremorne and during the sales campaign, sixty groups of buyers inspect the home and it sells to one of them. Two weeks later, I list another three-bedroom home in Cremorne and before the property goes online, I invite those buyers who are ready to buy now to a VIP preview of the new listing when the home is ready to go to market. If the home suits one of the VIP buyers, then they make an offer, begin negotiations and the home is often sold for a premium price before it is advertised online. This type of 'off-market' sale is more common than you think and may account for 20% or 30% of property transactions.

VIP previews are a valuable source of feedback for vendors as well. Buyers who are previewing your home are not shy to discuss its pros and cons or give feedback on price and presentation. It's a preview before you go to the market, so their feedback is valuable to ensure we are well positioned and priced competitively. Importantly, we may even get some feedback about competitive homes which are coming to market or have sold off market that we are not yet aware of.

STEP 2 – BUYERS AGENTS

Buyers agents are real estate agents who represent buyers rather than sellers. If you want to buy a property but you don't have the time to do all the legwork, or you don't know the area or the prices, then you should hire a buyers agent to do the work for you.

Buyers agents charge a 'success fee' to the buyer who hires them. There is no charge to the seller.

Every time a buyers agent signs a new client in my area, I receive an email of their client's brief, with a request to think about any property I may have seen recently that may meet that brief. If I have a match, I call them to discuss it further, and if the potential seller is agreeable then I will inspect that property with the buyers agent to see if it is in fact the right property for their client. We both do our homework first, to avoid wasting anyone's time.

For example, this is a typical buyers agent brief which may trigger a conversation and lead to an off-market sale.

Property type: Free-standing house

Budget: $3.5 to $5.5 million (up to $4 million if it needs work)

Location: Mosman (only the harbour side of Military Rd) and possibly Cremorne Point. They don't want Beauty Point area.

Specifics:

- Four bedrooms (or three double bedrooms plus a study)
- Must have two full bathrooms and an internal laundry
- They like gardening, so they want a decent block of at least 500 m^2
- They love character homes with good bones, high ceilings and period features
- Also open to modern or architect-designed homes
- Pool is neither here nor there for them
- Minimum one-off street garage or carport but preference for two-car parking
- Would renovate the right property (but need to factor that into their budget). They don't want to do a full DA, but will move walls, do bathrooms or kitchen updates
- The home has to be light, bright and airy with a good aspect
- They are open to a single or double level (but they don't want multiple levels)
- Preference for formal and informal living areas, separate area for their kids
- Ideally a good existing flow between internal and external living areas (or ability to create great outdoor entertaining)
- They prefer some sort of view or outlook but it is not essential.

With a buyer brief like this, I can narrow the search for a home down to within the nominated areas and budget, and perhaps even approach a suitable home owner to see if they might sell.

Importantly, buyers agents' briefs are a moving feast. The original brief may be changed after many weeks of searching without a result. The amended brief may allow me to revisit properties that were not considered first time round but would now solve the problem of finding a home.

It's important to say that I have never sold the perfect home! I have come close, but usually the buyer isn't happy with something, or so they say.

As many buyers agents are representing investors, they will also lease and manage those properties for their clients, again strengthening their relationship over time. Where that gets interesting for my clients is that, should I have a match of a buyer for your property and that buyer is an investor, then they are not going to be moving into the property. This means we can negotiate a deal to allow you to stay in your home and lease it back for a flexible term, which allows you time to look around and purchase again, without having to relocate twice.

The convenience of this type of sale cannot be overstated. You get to sell your property for a premium price, you get to bank the money and you still don't have to move out until you find your ideal next home and buy it. I have managed this type of sale on several occasions and sometimes it is the only way that a sale is going to happen.

Buyers agents are a great sounding board to help sellers understand current market value, as they are viewing properties with lots of agents. They are very connected to what is selling off market, not just the advertised homes. Many times, even I don't know that a property is for sale until it is reported sold.

STEP 3 – OPEN TIMES

Saturday is show day. Agents all over town have their properties scheduled for Saturday inspections. Whatever time you choose to show your property, it's very likely that another similar property will be open at the same time, and buyers may have to decide between the two properties as they cannot physically be in two places at once.

When buyers look at a property online, they look for reasons to rule it out. They can't see them all, so they need to prioritise their time. Your property needs to stand out and catch their eye for all the right reasons. Every time your agent lists another property, they need to fit it in to their existing schedule. Sometimes the open time you want is already taken.

The length of an open home may vary depending on the agent's schedule and prior commitments and the type and location of the property. If the agent has scheduled their opens for 30 minutes with 15 minutes' travel time in between properties, then they will need to fit yours into the same schedule. We allow 30 minutes between opens to be able to effectively set up and open a home. Buyers often arrive in the last five minutes, so we try not to rush everyone out right on closing time, but we need to stick to our schedule and lock the house, remove signage and drive to the next open home to do it all again.

When a property is harder to find or harder to park at, or involves three flights of stairs or a single elevator, then we allow 45 minutes for open homes to give buyers more time. If our schedule allows, we will stay a full 60 minutes. However, we have found over the years that with longer open times you rarely have more buyers inspect, they are just spread out over a longer period.

Most agents have their first inspection at 10 am, but the advantage of a 9 am open time may be that there are no other homes scheduled then. If no other home is open at the same time as your property, then buyers don't have to choose yours over another home. If they love your home so much, they may not bother seeing others later in the day. Buyers start out full of enthusiasm, so being the first inspection of the day has its merits. By midday, buyers are looking for a break to have some lunch, particularly if they have kids in tow. Sometimes, despite all the best intentions, they never get back into the swing of inspections again for the afternoon. Post-lunch fatigue sets in. Perhaps being first for the day is the best time of all.

Some properties lend themselves to twilight viewings. Be aware that the path and access to and from the house need to be well lit and signposted if you have a twilight open time, because buyers need to be able to negotiate the terrain with ease. Nothing would be worse than one of your buyers having a fall while trying to use their phone as a torch.

STEP 4 – OPEN INSPECTIONS

When you are planning your open home, think in terms of your eyes, ears and your nose.

Eyes

Start at the front door and walk through your property looking for things that may be out of place. Clear all benchtops so there is no clutter. If you have run out of time, just open a drawer and slide everything inside so it is out of sight. This goes for your easily transported valuables. While the incidence of theft is very rare at opens, it's best to remove the opportunity to avoid disappointment. Scan each room for phones, watches, jewellery, perfume, keys and other small valuables and put them safely out of sight or take them with you.

Ears

Check for any distracting noises. Don't put the washing machine or dryer on before you head out, and it's great to open windows and doors if there is no traffic noise. If you can, play some café-style music quietly in the background or ask your agent to bring their portable music system with them.

Nose

Did you cook fish in the kitchen last night? It may be too late now, as that smell hangs around, but keep it in mind for next week's open home. Do you have pets, litter trays or funny odours? A vanilla-scented candle can only do so much. Avoid taking a shower ten minutes before your agent arrives, too; the bathroom won't recover in time and buyers will know that you have rushed out.

Does your home, look, sound and smell like a sanctuary that buyers will fall in love with, or at the very least, is it 'neutral', so it does no harm?

It's a good idea to be gone before your agent arrives. If you do cross paths, be mindful that your agent is on a schedule of open homes for the day and they may not have much time to chat. They need to set up your home and some buyers always arrive early.

STEP 5 – EDITORIAL AND SOCIAL MEDIA

Your agent should be looking for the opportunity to provide editorial to the local paper. Local papers are always looking for newsworthy stories. Often the story is about the person who lived in the home or the architect who designed it or the location, not just the house. If your property has an unusual history, a wartime conversion, a past celebrity owner, a famous architect or a story to tell, then it deserves the chance to get editorial coverage.

Promoting your property on social media is another option as part of your marketing spend. In addition to your own social media accounts, you can tap into the audience behind corporate sites by purchasing one of their social media products as part of your media mix. For instance, Campaigntrack offers a product called AIM - Advanced Internet Marketing. AIM connects with active and passive buyers by promoting your property through their network using Google Search Ads, Google Display ads, Facebook ads, big data Facebook targeting and a unique property website with a custom URL.

Unlike newspaper advertising, online products offer different ways to measure visibility. They can track engagement, views, opens, click-throughs, alerts, shares, emails to the agent, phone-number reveals and downloads. There are also products available which retarget ads to potential buyers. Have you ever noticed that once you click on an ad for a pair of shoes it keeps following you around the internet, hoping you will click on it again?

STEP 6 – TEST IT FIRST

Before we launch your property on the major websites, we test it first on our own internal website.

Once you can see the layout, you can check punctuation, spelling, phrases and spacing to ensure your listing is how you like it. You can also check the sequence of photographs to ensure the 'hero' photo is your main shot and the other photos follow in logical order. The hero shot should be the photo that creates an immediate emotional response.

Each property has icons displaying the number of bedrooms, bathrooms and cars. Some websites allow additional icons for features such as a study or pool. Parking is always a little bit open to interpretation, as the icon is just a car, but can represent a lock-up garage, a carport or even a car space.

Our internal website is also where we post properties which are part of our private listings, so we can guide VIP buyers to inspect the property on our website before it is advertised to the public. Buyers should also monitor the office websites of agents they are actively working with to find those 'off-market' properties.

The off-market preview may run for a few days to a week or longer. We will send an email alert to our internal database of buyers who have consented to receive these from us for properties that match their buyer criteria. The computer checks all the buyers we have that match the specific property and it creates a mini brochure which is then sent directly to their inbox.

7. OPEN FOR BUSINESS

STEP 1 – LAUNCH THE PROPERTY ONLINE

Sellers often ask 'How quickly can we be on the market?' If we have a contract and agency sales agreement and the photos, floorplan and copy are completed and approved, then we can be online in 20 minutes.

The first open home can be any day of the week, however most properties start on a Saturday as that is the day most people will inspect - it makes sense to get started with a bang. Working backwards, then, it's important to give buyers a bit of a heads-up about your property so they can schedule to inspect it.

Ideally, your property is working to a timeline like this:

Monday - Photos, floorplan and copy completed. Marketing team at your property.

Tuesday - Checks and approvals. Backup day for photos in the event of rain.

Wednesday - Final approvals. Launch the property online, order the brochure and signboard.

Thursday - Initial buyer enquiry, signboard installed, brochure delivered to office.

Friday - Additional enquiry and backup day for brochure and signboard.

Saturday - First open home, lots of buyers have scheduled to inspect the property.

This timeline works for several reasons. It allows all the elements of the sale to come together in a timely manner, including third-party marketing components such as the brochure and signboard, and it offers buyers the opportunity to find the property, shortlist it for inspection and schedule time to inspect it on Saturday. It also allows a bit of wriggle room for weather and print or delivery delays if needed.

The buyers who inspect on the very first day are often the most motivated. They are actively looking and doing what serious buyers do, which is get out and inspect a property to see if it is right for them. It is very common to meet the final buyer of a property on the very first inspection day. Only an experienced agent will recognise them as the final buyer and nurture and hold onto them during the campaign to ensure they stay with the property. As you can imagine, over a three- or four-week campaign, many new homes will come on the market and even your very best buyer will inspect other homes. Unless they are in constant communication with your agent, then you won't know what their plans are.

Your agent's professional relationships with your buyers will determine the knowledge you have about your buyers and their level of interest in your home or someone else's home.

When a buyer makes an offer on your home, it may not be exclusive. In other words, they may have seen more than one home that suits them, and they may have made offers on several homes on the same day. Buyers like this expect an answer quickly, and often the seller who gets back to them the fastest will keep them as an active buyer. Your agent needs to keep them engaged and negotiating, not just give them a yes or a no to their offer. The buyer will appreciate a fast response, even if it is just to ask a question about their offer, because they will recognise that the seller is considering their offer and has not dismissed it. Even if the offer is not at the level the seller expects, your agent should be working with that buyer to increase their offer before they buy another property. Remember, time kills deals, so agents who engage and negotiate early will do more deals.

STEP 2 – DATABASE BUYER MATCH

Every time a buyer enquires about a property online or we physically meet them at an open home, with their permission we collect their details so that we can help them to buy the ideal property. We transfer their contact information into our CRM (Customer Relationship Management) software so that every buyer has their own individual profile, which allows us to service them better. Any communication includes an 'opt out' link, so we are only dealing with buyers who want our assistance.

As I enter a buyer or confirm that they have inspected a particular property, I send them a text to thank them for inspecting the home. It's a courtesy text as a genuine thank you, but I do also ask if they have further interest in the property. I ask if they would like additional information, such as the strata report or even a contract of sale. All they do is text their email address back and I will forward that information to them. Many people are grateful not just for the immediate follow up but also for providing them with relevant additional information.

When I am selling an apartment with a price guide of $600,000 and 30 buyers inspect it, each buyer receives a courtesy phone call from us to again thank them for inspecting, and to ask them for some feedback about the property and whether it suits them or not.

If they like the property, we then need to flag that and start a conversation around buying this home. If the property doesn't suit, then we ask what buying criteria is most important to them so we can help match them with another property. The more we know about the buyer, the better the matches we can offer them.

To effectively manage a buyer, we look at a broad range of criteria, starting with the basics and moving to the specific. The information is broken into categories to help with searches. We aim to include all the details shown opposite.

With this information, we can search other potential property listings we have to see if they match any buyers. If you want to buy a property for up to $600,000, then you won't want to receive notifications about houses for $4 million, and we don't want to send you the wrong property information either.

Title ____________________

First name ____________________

Surname ____________________

Partner or spouse details ____________________

Mobile phone number ____________________

Home number ____________________

Email address ____________________

Home address ____________________

The ideal buyer criteria categories include the following:

Active buyer - Yes ☐ or No ☐

Property type - House ☐ or Strata ☐

Price Min. __________ and Max. __________

Beds ________ No. required

Baths ________ No. required

Car parking ________ No. required

Suburbs ____________________
(Nominate the suburbs or postcodes that they are interested in hearing about.)

Recently, I listed a two-bedroom apartment in Mosman and about 60 buyers inspected over a short period. One buyer shared her ideal criteria with me, including naming several streets that she had strong interest in. A short time later, I listed a two-bedroom apartment in one of her nominated streets. As a VIP active buyer who was working with me, I was able to introduce her to the property with a small select group of active buyers before the property was listed online. The home was exactly what she was after and after a short negotiation the owner accepted a strong offer to secure the apartment without any marketing expenses. Contracts were exchanged with 42 days settlement, which meant the owner would receive their payment about a month earlier than if the property had gone through a four-week auction campaign. It was a win/win for both my clients.

STEP 3 – FIRST SATURDAY OPEN HOME

Preparation for your first open home starts the week before, not the morning of.

If you launch your property online on a Wednesday afternoon for the first open home on the Saturday afternoon, buyers have had at least two full days to find out about it. Many buyers set themselves up for email alerts on the main websites, while many others simply rely on looking online on a Thursday or Friday while they are at work. Many employers don't realise how much time their staff spend looking for a home on their time! Thursdays and Fridays during work hours are the most popular times for buyers to put together their shortlist of homes to inspect on Saturday. If you don't launch your property online until Friday afternoon, buyers have a lot less time to find your home and plan their inspections. You will likely have less buyers than had you launched on Wednesday.

How many buyers will inspect at an open home? It depends on the market and your marketing spend. The number of buyers who physically inspect your home will vary for many reasons. You might expect your very first open to have the highest number of potential buyers, and sometimes it will. Sometimes the number of buyers is lower than expected, and that is a big red flag that something isn't right. If everything else checks out as correct, then the issue will be price.

Buyers won't inspect a home that doesn't appear to be good value. If it feels over-priced they will stay away; conversely, if it appears under-priced, many buyers tell me they don't bother to inspect because they believe it will sell for much more. Getting the price guide right is that important: you may never know how many potential buyers you lose by pricing your property too high or too low.

On any Saturday, we may have from four to eight open homes. Our schedule may look like this:

9:00 - 9:30	Harrison St, Cremorne
10:00 - 10:30	Harriette St, Neutral Bay
11:00 - 11:30	David Street, Crows Nest
12:00 - 12:30	Carter Street, Cammeray
1:00 - 1:30	Benelong Road, Cremorne

2:00 - 2:30 Avenue Road, Mosman

3:00 - 3:30 Muston Street, Mosman

We know that buyers are working to a schedule too. We know that buyers will try and maximise their time at a property, and there will always be buyers who turn up a little bit early and some who are running a little bit late. We try and be open a little bit early and stay a little bit late as well, but when it's time to pack up and get to the next open home, that's what we do.

When we are about to open the front door, I like to text the owner a photo to show that we are ahead of time and that the open house is, in fact, open. It's visual accountability in action, showing them that we are doing what we said we will do. I recently sold an apartment that was on the market for ten weeks. I did open home inspections mid-week and on Saturdays for ten weeks straight and texted the owner a photo or video of every single open home as a reminder that I was there as I said I would be. Some days no one inspected at all, but that didn't change the fact that I was there waiting to meet the potential buyer twice a week and the owner knew that. When the property sold, the owner told me she appreciated the consistent reminders that I was working hard to sell her apartment, even when no one inspected.

If your open home is the last inspection time of the day, then we will extend it for as long as the buyers need. If, however, a buyer arrives after the inspection time and we are on our way to another open home, we will get their details and offer them another inspection at a later date, either at the end of the day or on Sunday, depending on the arrangements we already have with the seller for that weekend.

On a sunny beach-going Saturday in our area, the traffic can be terrible. It can take 20 minutes to go 2 kilometres, so we are mindful of where we are going next, and the traffic conditions on the day and the available parking at the next location.

STEP 4 – DATA ENTRY, SMS FOLLOW UP

When we open six or more open homes on a Saturday, we are going to meet at least 30 people (but often 60 people), and some homes on their first day of inspection will attract 20 or more groups. That means we could have met up to 100 buyers on a busy Saturday.

Some buyers inspect homes on their own, so we can take their name and number and make a mental note or write ourselves a note to remind us who they were when we go to call them back. Other buyers inspect properties in groups. When four people arrive at the front door at the same time, they can either be all individual buyers, two groups of two or one group of four. It's a question I need to ask so I can ensure I don't miss any buyers and everyone feels welcomed and important. We identify the buyer in the group who is the decision-maker, and whose contact details represent that group, although we may also make a note that mum and dad inspected as well.

In addition to our open home books, where we physically write names and numbers of buyers and make notes, we can enter buyers' details directly into our client list online via our database software. We can also identify registered buyers who use the online system. I find that I remember names and faces best when I meet a person and write their name down and check the spelling with them face to face.

In between open homes, we either call or send a video or text to our owners to tell them the number of buyers who inspected and any standout comments or buyers, so they aren't kept waiting until the end of the day to hear from us. After our scheduled inspections we may have second inspections and perhaps additional buyer appointments. Then we head back to the office to do the paperwork. Depending on the type of day we have had, we may have entered all the buyers into our database from our phone or we may have had our virtual assistant in the Philippines enter them for us. Having a virtual assistant allows us to focus on dealing with buyers and sellers face to face, while much of the background paperwork and compliance tasks are performed out of office.

Everyone who inspects a home with us is included in our client list and receives a text message (SMS) on the same day to thank them for viewing the property. We also offer them a strata report or contract if they text back their email address. If a buyer texts back requesting a contract, then I will call them to acknowledge that request straight away and they go to the top of the list as a 'contract holder' and 'hot prospective buyer'.

Buyers may have inspected four or five properties in a row on a Saturday. By the afternoon, they are exhausted and can hardly remember one property from the next. Most agents wait until Monday or Tuesday to call buyers back. I call late on Saturday afternoon for two reasons. One, most buyers remember who I am and the property that they looked at, as they received a thank-you text only an hour or so earlier. Some are enjoying an afternoon drink with a friend and I am the only agent who has contacted them since their inspections that morning. They have received a text and a call from me, and I may get valuable feedback straight away. Some buyers tell me that they still haven't decided or discussed it yet, while others are ready to make an offer.

If I don't reach them, then I leave a message to say that I will call them back on Monday. If I do reach the buyer, I may have an offer to take to the owner with which to start a conversation. We may speak several times on Sunday and by Monday, we may have an agreement and I write up the sales advice and send it through to their conveyancer.

Importantly, everyone who inspects the property is given the same opportunity. There is often one buyer who is much more motivated to purchase straight away than any other buyer and my role is to help that to happen. I like to keep the momentum because I am aware that time kills deals.

STEP 5 – CALL BACKS AND FEEDBACK TO THE OWNER

We hold scheduled inspections mid-week and on Saturdays. Mid-week inspections are held on either Wednesdays or Thursdays, during the day or at the end of the day. Often no one will attend mid-week inspections, which is why end-of-day inspections make more sense. Buyers who can't attend an open home at 10:30 am because they are at work, can often arrange to leave work early to inspect a property at 5 pm or 5:30 pm, and everyone can make a 6 pm inspection, so end-of-day inspections are better attended than early in the day mid-week opens.

The best time to get quality feedback from a buyer who has inspected a property is the same day they inspected it. The very best time is to discuss the property with the buyer while they are still at the property. Depending on the number of buyers we have at a property, we will either have time for a good chat with a buyer or not. If we do have time, then engaging with buyers while they are in a prospective property will ensure the very best feedback.

Importantly, I am not fishing for negative feedback simply to give the owner a list of things buyers may not like. I am, however, trying to uncover things about the property that aren't quite right for them, that perhaps I can help make happen for them.

The value of feedback is to help the seller appreciate the buyer's perspective and, together with the agent, to try to find a solution that brings a deal together. One buyer gave me the feedback that the property was too close to the freeway and therefore too noisy. I couldn't move the property and I couldn't move the freeway but I had already invited a specialist in double-glazing to provide a quote. I was able to show the buyer that there are window treatment products that would help reduce the noise and they were less expensive than the buyer had imagined.

Once this cost was factored into the offer, the owner was still delighted with the price and the deal moved forward. A year later when I visited the property again, the buyer had not made any change to the windows. When I asked why, they simply said they got used to the noise and it wasn't so bad after all. When a property is next to a freeway, it will be noisier than some other apartments, but it will still find a buyer or a tenant at a price. Once that price is understood, the property is sold or leased.

Some buyers understand that their feedback will assist the agent to discuss the pros and cons of the property. Constructive feedback helps a deal move forward. I have never sold the perfect home and I encourage buyers to talk to me about what concerns them, so we can look at how to solve that problem for them. Sometimes a problem can't be overcome, which means that the property is just not the right match for the buyer.

If a buyer inspects a two-bedroom apartment because the price is right for them, but they really need a three-bedroom place, it just won't work. The only solution is to move to another, less expensive area where the three-bedroom apartments are in their budget. Once I have this feedback, I can do two things. One is to tell the owner that that buyer isn't our ideal buyer so we can let them go. The other is to help that buyer by introducing them to another agent in a different area who may be able to help them.

Buyer feedback helps the agent and the seller to price their home correctly. If every buyer likes the property and there are no issues other than the price, then that's great feedback. The price is the problem. The seller can decide to do nothing, hoping for a 'wood duck' to come along, or they can drop the price so it is more competitive with other homes on the market in order to attract offers. It's great news for an agent to be able to go back to buyers who have inspected and tell them, 'The owner is listening to the feedback and has made a price adjustment to meet the market'. Buyers can't help but jump in with an offer and that's how a conversation around price leads to a sale above market.

STEP 6 – JUST LISTED, DLs DELIVERED

When buyers come to an open home inspection, we ask them for their name, number and postcode. Some will ask 'Why do you want my postcode?' If they are from out of the area, then they may not be familiar with the location and the surrounding amenities. As I explained in chapter 5, step 12, we offer a community feature sheet handout that helps them appreciate the benefits of the suburb and why it is so highly sought-after. We want to help them compete with the locals by understanding what the locals already know - that this is a great property in a great location.

If they are from the local area, then they may be a neighbour, or they may be looking to upgrade or downsize in their local area. They may already live in and love the suburb, but they are looking for a lifestyle change. They may need to sell their existing home first to purchase this one or they may be looking for an investment property in their familiar territory. When we know the buyer's postcode, we can have a better conversation with them about their reasons for viewing today; remember my first question, 'Are you buying or browsing today?'

As part of our marketing plan for your home, we took wonderful photographs which are now online, so active buyers who are looking online can find your home and fall in love with it. But what about the passive buyers who already live in and love the neighbourhood but who may not be looking online to find a new home? As part of your marketing mix of products, we may print 2,000 double-sided colour DL-size brochures announcing your home is for sale. The reason we do this is to deliver them around the suburb to get the attention of those passive buyers who already appreciate your neighbourhood and who may be thinking of moving, but are not actively looking. Suddenly they find a DL brochure in their letterbox telling them that your home is available for sale. What we didn't know is that they have always admired your home when they have driven past and have always had interest to buy it, only it hasn't been for sale. Now is their chance to make a move. The DL brochure in their letterbox has done the trick.

Neighbours buy homes in your area too, plus neighbours also have friends and family who they want to help move into their area. It makes sense to let the neighbours know that your home is on the market so they can invite their friends to come and see it at the next open home. I often tell sellers that not only do neighbours buy homes, but it's the perfect opportunity for them to choose their new neighbours by inviting friends to inspect.

A 'Just Listed' DL brochure might be considered junk mail by some home-owners, but not by those who want to buy your house. To them, it's the reason they found out your house was for sale. We never know where your buyer is going to come from but we do know where to fish to find them, so the DL letterbox cards could be your local area heroes.

Our local council defines junk mail as newspaper circulars such as those from supermarket chains, while they categorise information from real estate agents as community information, not junk mail. Not all residents see it that way, so we do our best to avoid any letterbox with a 'No junk mail' warning. Better to be safe than sorry.

STEP 7 – DATABASE AND ENQUIRY FOLLOW UP

Now that we have had our first Saturday open home and your agent has followed up all the buyers on Saturday and again on Monday, that's not all we can do. The truth is that more than half the buyers I call back will not answer their phone, either on Saturday or on Monday. That's why I start with a thank-you text as a first line of follow up - and it puts my name and phone number in their phone along with a positive message. The phone call I make on Saturday may result in one of these outcomes:

- My phone call is answered by the buyer and we have a valuable chat about your property.

- My phone call is answered by the buyer and they haven't had time to think about it.
- My phone call is answered by the buyer's partner who says they are not available.
- My phone call is answered and they tell me they can't talk now, they are in a meeting.
- My phone call is answered and they tell me it's a wrong number, don't call back.
- My phone call is not answered and goes to regular voicemail and I leave a message.
- My phone call is not answered and I leave a ten-second voice message.
- My phone call is not answered and my ten-second message is converted to text.
- My phone call is not answered and the message says don't leave a message, send me a text.
- My phone call is not answered and I can't leave a message because the mailbox is full.
- My phone call is not answered and I find out that the number is not connected.

If 20 people inspected your home on Saturday morning, by Saturday afternoon I will have texted them all and called them all but probably only spoken to five of them. On Monday morning I try again, and of the fifteen, I may speak to three and leave messages when I can. On Monday afternoon I may have had one person call me back and I call the other eleven and speak to five. By Tuesday I try the other six again and leave messages when I can, and may speak to three and never hear from the other three again. If I have 20 people to call, I can guarantee I will never be able to speak to every one of them. I do however send one text and make three calls, and if I have their details on email, I will send an email to try and get feedback and see how best to help them as buyers.

By Wednesday, we have another open home inspection, so the cycle begins again. Sometimes after a few days of trying to reach a buyer who inspected, when I finally catch them, they completely deny ever inspecting the property at all, so I thank them for their time and wish them well.

Call backs are the business end of real estate. I love the challenge. Some buyers are looking for all the help they can get from the agent and I will do my best for them, even if this property is not for them. They are able to give me constructive feedback and a solid buyer brief, and I can set up a buyer alert in our database so that when I list another property that may be suitable for them, they will automatically receive an email alert from me inviting them to inspect, whether it is 'off market' or 'on market'.

Some buyers think they don't need a real estate agent's help, and they will never know the properties they have just missed out on.

STEP 8 – FIRST MID-WEEK OPEN FOR INSPECTION

Your home has now been on the market for its 'off-market' preview and then listed online as part of our full sales campaign. Your first open inspection was a great success, with 20 buyers arriving to have a look at your home. The follow ups have been solid and email alerts have gone out to the database. DL flyers have been delivered in the neighbourhood and your half-page or full-page advertisement has been placed in the local paper, which will be delivered on Wednesday night and Thursday morning across the area.

Your first mid-week open is down for Thursday lunchtime so that as many buyers as possible will see the ad in the paper and find the time to pop in for a look. As it's early daylight savings and it gets dark at 5:30 pm, we are going for a lunchtime viewing instead of an evening one - the property is not easily accessed in the dark and the pathway is a bit uneven. Mid-week inspections are for everyone but are mainly viewed by locals who aren't working, although buyers may travel a few suburbs to inspect without the Saturday crowds. The kids are at school, so one or other parent may be able to inspect, if the open time doesn't clash with their scheduled tennis, golf or coffee appointment.

Mid-week opens can attract good buyer numbers or you get no one at all! They are rarely in between. We may have good second inspections; good inspections by partners who couldn't do Saturday because of kids' sport or their own sport or their own travel; good inspections from buyers from

Melbourne, Canberra or the mid-North Coast; or we may have just one or two neighbours or no one at all. It's a lottery. The more the property is marketed, however, the more likely we are to have successful mid-week inspections. It's never a waste of time, it's just part of the process, and I know from experience that it takes only one buyer to inspect and make an offer to get the sale underway.

STEP 9 – CALL BACKS, DISCUSSION AND FEEDBACK

After every open home, we text and call the buyers who inspected to thank them and get some feedback. Whether it's one person or ten people, the process is the same. We call buyers back the same day asking for meaningful feedback.

If your property is not right for them, we can steer them in the direction of another property. Despite what some sellers think, I can't talk the uninterested buyer into buying your home. I don't have a magic spell that suddenly makes them want to change their mind and buy a property that doesn't suit them. I can however discuss the advantages of your home over other homes that they may be looking at, and that's where the constant contact comes into play.

Even if they say your home doesn't suit them, if they tell me what else they are considering, I can help them compare homes, locations and prices. It may be that after they look at several other homes, your home is in fact a better fit for them than anything else on the market. That's why I persist in contacting them to see if there is a future match, even if they say 'Not right now'.

If your property is of interest to a buyer, we talk them through the pros and cons, looking for the opportunity to offer a second inspection so that they can take any other decision-makers. If a second inspection at a scheduled open time doesn't work for all decision-makers, then I like to offer a private inspection at a time to suit them. This could be at 7:30 am on their way to work. It could be that they leave work at lunchtime to have a look at 12:30 pm or it could be an after-work inspection at 6 pm or 7 pm or 8 pm. If they have agreed to a second inspection, then we will drop everything to get the buyers back to your property so we can advance the connection.

I may never get the opportunity to discuss the property with one or two of the buyers again. Sometimes they literally were just walking past at the open time and decided to have a stickybeak. If they tell me, then at least I know, but some buyers who inspect just don't want any further contact and will not say why or return calls. After I've left three messages, I let them go. When a buyer isn't calling me back with questions, it is generally a sign that they are no longer interested - generally, but not always. Sometimes when I call a buyer back a week later, they tell me they have been away since last weekend and do have some further interest but were out of town. Sometimes they have a big deal going on at work and just didn't have the time to commit to the property. That deal is done and now they have the time, so persistence pays dividends.

I log all my phone calls to buyers and make sure I give them every opportunity to respond. By keeping a history of buyer inspections and feedback, I can build a better understanding of how to help buyers in the future. It also gives me solid feedback to discuss with the seller.

The buyer and seller communication during the sales process is the most important thing of all. An agent may be able pull a deal together from a buyer with slight interest if they were diligent in chasing them for constructive feedback and asking the right questions.

STEP 10 – TARGET BUYER APPOINTMENTS AND SECOND INSPECTIONS

Part way into a sales campaign, I have a list of buyers who have inspected the property and my goal is to find out what their ongoing interest in the property is. This only happens with a genuine exchange of information, either on the phone or face to face. If a buyer has some interest, then my goal is to get them back for a second inspection. Not only does this give them an opportunity to view the property again, but it gives me the chance to ask them relevant questions to find out where they are in the buyer's cycle. Have they just sold their property, have they bid and missed at auction recently, do they need to sell before they buy? There are lots of different scenarios that will affect their timing and motivation to purchase this home if it is mostly right for them.

In discussing the pros and cons of every property with a buyer, I tell them what I know to be true. While I have sold hundreds of homes, I have never sold the perfect home. Every home is a buyer's compromise, but if it is 70% right then I focus on that, rather than thinking it is 30% wrong. If you can tick seven out of ten boxes, then this home could well be the best match you will find on the market today.

During this stage of marketing your home, we are also meeting other buyers at other homes, some like yours and some different. The same is true for all the agents working in our office. As they are showing their homes, they are meeting buyers as well. Some will like their homes and others are looking for something else. That something else might be your home, so I make sure I discuss your property with all the other agents in our office to try and find a targeted buyer match. If we know of a certain buyer who has looked at another home and isn't interested, but may be interested in yours, I will call them and invite them to have a look. Depending on what we know about them, we may even insist that they come and have a look. Buyers we are working with respond well to our recommendations and they trust us, so they will likely come and have a look at your home. Many times, that buyer will say, 'I didn't think this would suit us but it is so much better than I thought', and the next thing that happens is they want a second inspection and a deal is done.

STEP 11 – CONTINUE OPEN HOMES, CALL BACKS AND FEEDBACK

We continue our scheduled open homes mid-week and on Saturdays, plus we line up as many second inspections as we can. I want buyers to focus on your home. They will either love it more on the second or third inspection or they will lose interest. Either way we have given them the option of buying your home. It may be right for them or they may move on, but the trust we build with the buyer remains. When we are selling another home in two weeks' time and we call them to say, 'I'd like you to take a look at this home, I think it will work for you', they will respond favourably.

When we target a buyer and invite them to consider homes they have not seen, it builds trust in our relationship. The buyer must feel that we are looking out for them - and we are. They don't feel obligated in any way, however they do feel that it is an opportunity that we are sending them and it could be the one! If they are a genuine buyer, then they have nothing to lose.

Buyers can choose the real estate agent they want to work with on off-market deals but once a home is listed, they then need to deal with the agent who is selling it. Sometimes, buyers come back to us to ask advice on how to deal with a competitor agent who just doesn't connect with buyers. It's a big mistake to put the wrong agent in front of the right buyer. It will cost the seller dearly.

We have a weekly sales meeting on Wednesday mornings with all our agents and much of that meeting is spent discussing the buyers we have met and trying to match them with other properties that we are selling but that they have not seen. Bear in mind that a buyer looking at a $4 million house may have also told us that they are hoping to help one of their children to buy an apartment in the area as well. This is such valuable information and allows us to target them as buyers with either off-market listings or new listings that they have not yet seen. That's the value of a great office with a great team of agents who support each other to get deals done.

8. NEGOTIATION

STEP 1 – FIRST OFFER AND START NEGOTIATIONS

We're just mid-way through our four-week auction campaign and we have had two Saturday opens, two mid-week opens, and we are starting our third week of the campaign. One of the buyers I targeted has already had a second inspection. They are telling me that the home ticks a few boxes for them and that they would like to make an offer. We have a guide price of $1,400,000 to $1,500,000 with the auction in two Saturdays' time. The buyer has decided to make an offer prior to the auction to try and secure the property now. There may be many reasons for this decision, here are just a few:

- This buyer may have been to an auction recently and seen that it was well attended, and the registered bidders participated and bid competitively such that the property sold in excess of the price guide.

- This buyer may have been an observer at an auction, just getting a feel for the market.
- This buyer may have registered to bid at an auction and did bid but still missed out. It always seems like there is someone with more money than you at an auction. They don't want to go through the emotion of another auction. They believe that negotiating prior will be less stressful.
- This buyer may not be available to attend the auction in two weeks, so they want to buy it now. They don't want to bid on the phone or send a friend along to bid for them.
- This buyer may not like auctions and has said that they will not attend the auction if it goes ahead so they simply want to pay a fair price for the property now.

There are many reasons why a buyer decides to make an offer prior to auction.

However, it may be that the seller has instructed the agent not to accept any offers prior to auction. That is their choice. They may also instruct the agent not to accept any offers in the first week or the first two weeks. It's the owner's house and the owner's sale so they make the rules. The agent will certainly give their opinion based on their experience and the current buyers, but it's the owner's decision.

My seller has already told me they will consider all offers prior to auction so I am working with the buyer to put their best foot forward.

When a buyer makes an offer on a property, their first offer will rarely be their best offer, despite what they say.

Some buyers will impose unreasonable restrictions on their offer. For instance one buyer told me, 'I want to make an offer, the offer is $X and that's my final offer, you have until five o'clock this afternoon to take my offer or I will withdraw it'.

That's not a negotiation in my book, it's a demand and few people respond well to demands. When a buyer behaves in this manner it could be their ego, it could be inexperience or it could be that they had a bad experience with another agent in the past. My role is to open a conversation with them around the offer amount and how they came to choose that specific figure. I suggest we park the five o'clock deadline and discuss the offer first. I am particularly looking for confirmations around finance approvals, building inspections, settlement period, how the deposit will be paid, what amount of deposit will be paid and the date for unconditional exchange.

Often the buyer has not considered any of these variables, each one of which forms part of the offer for the seller's consideration. The buyer often just focuses on the price. If you call their bluff and say, 'OK, and we will exchange unconditionally at 5 pm today', they will likely back-pedal making a lot of noise, because they know they can't be ready in that timeframe anyway. Let me say that in my experience, buyer-imposed deadlines are not helpful to anyone in terms of getting the deal done.

By law, the real estate agent must submit every offer that a buyer makes to the seller. If a buyer calls me and makes an offer over the phone, I log the details of the call and the offer, however I also ask them to email me the offer in writing.

It's not essential they do this, because neither their verbal offer nor their email offer is binding. The only offer that is binding is one that is followed up by actions. Those actions are to write the offer on the contract of sale and have it signed off by both parties along with the 66W waiving the cooling off period from the conveyancer and a bank cheque for the agreed 10% of the purchase price which is then exchanged and dated. No other offer is binding.

I ask buyers to put their offer in writing, though, because it gives me an opportunity to discuss that offer with them before they put it in writing. Often I can negotiate a better offer than the original offer they called me with and their confirmation of this is the email they send me. They need to also include agreement on settlement time and deposit amount and any other variables that they are requesting.

As the agent, I can't vary the contract, so when a buyer (or their conveyancer) wants a change to the contract it must be through the seller's conveyancer who will seek instructions from the seller. Buyers who simply throw a number at the agent over the phone need to consider all the elements of the sale and confirm them in writing to avoid any misunderstanding. If the buyer says one figure and the owner accepts, then the buyer can argue that he had offered less and then there is going to be a problem. The written offer should always come from the buyer and the agent will seek confirmation of the details from the buyer.

Buyers and sellers may only buy or sell a property several times in their lives. Real estate agents could sell a home every day, so they are far more knowledgeable about the way things are done. It's the agent's role to guide the buyer, whether they are a first-home buyer or a seasoned home buyer, to help them put their offer together, so that it is attractive to the seller and it has the best chance of success.

STEP 2 – PRESENT THE OFFER TO THE OWNER

I keep saying that 'Time kills deals', so I am mindful that I need to submit any negotiated offer to the owner in a reasonable time. However, at the same time, a first offer is just not going to do it. There may be other buyers who are ready to make an offer but may be waiting for auction day. In 100% of cases, every owner's response to a buyer's first offer is the same: 'Will they pay any more?'

The second part of the seller's response should be, and often is, 'Are there any other buyers who will pay more?' I now have the chance to go back to the buyer who made the offer and all the other buyers who have inspected the property who may have ongoing interest to try and find out what they would pay.

When I call the buyer who made the original offer, it's a good news conversation. The owner has not said no to their offer, they have simply asked if the buyer can pay a bit more. Naturally, the buyer may get defensive and say that their offer is a good offer in the current climate. They may even start telling me all the things that are wrong with the property. It's part of the process to let them have their say. Some buyers need to vent. At the right moment, I encourage them to park those thoughts and focus on the home and help them to see themselves living there in a year's time.

Once they have reconnected with the home, the conversation will come back to either buying the home or missing out. If they are intent on buying it with an offer prior to auction, then the seller is looking for a premium price. The buyer is looking to pay market price without competition, but that's not the way this sale is going to play out. The buyer will usually say, 'Let me talk to my other half and get back to you'.

As the seller, you trust your agent to deliver the good news and the bad news. Your agent should tell you exactly the feedback they receive and pass on all offers whether they are high or low. A buyer who missed out on a property asked me once, 'How do I know the agent has submitted my offer?' While agents are required by law to submit all offers, as that buyer says, how do you know?

Meantime, I call all the other interested parties. Buyers with interest have usually asked for a contract of sale but it's not a hard and fast rule, so I will call all buyers who have inspected to give them an update on the sale. The update is that we have received an offer from a buyer prior to auction and the owner is considering the offer.

That's all I say. Of course, the first response from every buyer is 'Well, can you tell me what the offer is?' Unfortunately, no, I can't tell you what the offer is because that was a private conversation between that buyer and myself. I operate on the understanding that their conversation is protected under the *Privacy Act 1988*. In this Act, section 14 stipulates privacy rights known as the Information Privacy Principles (IPPs). Essentially, the buyer who made the offer has not given me their consent to share that offer with anyone else. The other side of the coin is that I also respect every buyer's rights to privacy, and if they make an offer then I will not reveal that amount to any other buyer either, without their express permission.

Some buyers appreciate my position and others can't believe it because they have been on the wrong end of other real estate agents shopping their offers around in the past, and have been, in their words, 'gazumped by unscrupulous agents'. It should be remembered that shopkeepers take orders, while real estate agents negotiate.

I will then say something along these lines: 'That buyer has the same information about the property as you do and they have made up their own mind and made an offer without reference to you or any other buyer, so I suggest you do exactly the same thing and make the very best offer you are comfortable with. If you should miss out then at least you know that you gave it your very best shot and submitted your walk-away price'.

Importantly, the owner has given me instructions to seek all offers prior to the auction, however I am not running an auction before the auction by telling you that I have an offer of $1,000 so that you can offer $1 more with an expectation that I will go back and forth until only one buyer remains. That's not what I am here to do. I am here to ask you to submit your best and final offer in an email to me, so the owner can decide if they wish to accept an offer now or take the property to auction. It's the owner's decision.

The result is that I either receive a premium offer that the seller is delighted with from a motivated buyer who is prepared to exchange contracts straight away, and the property is sold, or the offers are not at a level that the seller will accept at this stage of the campaign, in which case the property continues on its scheduled path to auction.

STEP 3 – NEGOTIATE TO AGREE ON TERMS, PRICE, DEPOSIT, SETTLEMENT DATE AND FINAL PRICE

In the event that I have been able to successfully negotiate with the buyer making an offer prior to the auction, and the buyer has proposed a premium price that the seller would be delighted to accept prior to auction, we have a reached a point of 'O & A' or 'Offer & Acceptance'. This essentially means that the buyer and the seller have, through the actions and skill of the real estate agent, agreed in principle on the price, the settlement terms and the amount of the deposit.

The real estate agent will then issue a Sales Advice Notice to both conveyancers. This notice summarises the agreed price and terms and introduces the two conveyancers to each other so that they can finalise the contract. The buyer's conveyancer will direct questions about the property and the contract terms back to the seller's conveyancer and, depending on how long this takes, time kills deals. If either side is not responding promptly and actively working to agree on terms, the deal can falter.

If the property were to go to auction, then there would be no cooling off period on auction day and the seller is looking for the same conditions to sell prior to auction. However, the buyer may be seeking a cooling off period to finalise their due diligence or obtain formal bank approval. If the seller allows a cooling off period, then the property is 'under offer' and no further inspections are permitted, so the property is effectively 'in limbo' for five business days. This is not an advantage to the seller in the week leading up to a scheduled auction so it is highly unlikely that the seller will agree to allow a cooling off period.

Contract clauses are then negotiated, and requests can be sent back and forward until both sides agree or disagree. At this point, there is no binding agreement yet, so either party can change their mind and walk away.

STEP 4 – CROSS-CHECK WITH ALL BUYERS WHO INSPECTED

While we have identified a buyer who is working with us to secure the property, the property has not yet sold and the buyer or the seller can still change their mind at any time and for any reason.

Some agents will sit back and cross their arms, thinking to themselves, 'My job is done', but what if another buyer has just decided that they are now ready to buy the property before auction? The agent needs to cross-check with all buyers to see if anyone else is ready to purchase and at what price and terms they are considering buying the property.

The agent needs to call all possible buyers and advise them that an offer has been made on the property, and the owners are looking to sell prior to auction. Every buyer will ask the question, 'What's the offer?' and in my mind, a good agent will advise them that the offer is confidential, however if they do have an interest in buying the home would they please submit their very best offer by email for the owner's consideration.

If the buyer knows the offer amount, they are not going to put forward their very best offer; they will simply put forward an offer that is slightly higher than the offer that is already under consideration. If the agent goes back and forth between buyers revealing the offer each time, then they are effectively running an auction before the scheduled auction - not negotiating the best price from all interested buyers.

Buyers quickly tire of what they call 'Dutch auction' tactics and pull out of negotiation, meaning the buyer who would have paid the most at auction has now walked away and the sale has lost its competitive edge, which has likely cost the seller thousands and thousands of dollars.

The agent's skill and process in managing a pre-auction offer can be the difference between a record price and just another sale.

STEP 5 – IF NOT SOLD, CONTINUE TO AUCTION

In this instance, the buyer has decided not to follow through with the pre-auction offer. It could be that they are not comfortable with a response to a clause in the contract, they could not get a cooling off period or they might simply have changed their mind. Perhaps this isn't the house for them after all, particularly at that price. Perhaps they think they will pick the house up for less at auction. There is no binding agreement, so they simply walk away. It's a bitter pill for the seller to swallow, as they had hoped to have the sale all wrapped up before auction day, but it is not to be.

The open home inspections have continued during the discovery stage, because regardless of negotiation, the property stays on the market until a binding contract has been exchanged. The buyer is not disclosing if they plan to attend and bid at the auction now, although two new buyers have shown good interest and expressed their intention to attend the auction.

When a buyer has good interest in a property, they will request a copy of the contract of sale and a building report. When a buyer engages their own building inspector to make their own checks it is a good sign, they are more than just interested. The agent makes the home available at a time to suit the building inspector and in this case the buyer also attends the home to ask the inspector about the property as he does his rounds.

The buyer's conveyancer then sends some questions to the seller's conveyancer, and let's say in this case they have requested a 5% deposit instead of the usual 10% if they are the successful purchasers at auction. This usually indicates that the buyer has 5% available in cash to pay the deposit now, while the balance of their funds may be invested in a term deposit account so is not immediately available.

9. AUCTION

STEP 1 – SETTING THE SCENE

The auction is fast-approaching and the agent has a shortlist of buyers with some level of interest but no stand-out buyer at this stage. Buyers are playing their cards close to their chest, so it is difficult to read how things might play out on auction day.

Ideally, on the Thursday afternoon or evening, after the mid-week inspection, the agent will meet with the sellers to sit down and discuss the response to the campaign and possible outcomes. This is an important meeting to set the scene for Saturday's on-site auction and to anticipate what may or may not happen.

There are several ways the auction could go, depending on who turns up on the day. There could be:

- no interested buyers at all
- interested buyers who don't register to bid

- one registered bidder
- two or more registered bidders.

It's important to remember that auction day is part of the process. We have been in campaign mode for almost four weeks now, with the opportunity to sell at any stage prior to auction to any buyer who was ready to negotiate with a strong fear of missing out, if the property went to auction.

In this case that didn't happen, so we are now approaching auction day and the opportunity to sell unconditionally under the hammer. If that doesn't happen, then we move to post-auction negotiations and then to the property being transferred to a private treaty sale next week.

The agent's setting-the-scene meeting with the sellers will attempt to identify which buyers are our most likely bidders and who may be our most likely buyer. If buyers have given us any indication of their budget, we consider that feedback and any other information available to us.

The seller is asked to complete and sign the auction reserve letter for the auctioneer. They will write down three figures:

- Seller's bid (vendor bid) in case there are no opening bids or in case it can be used to encourage additional bidding
- Auction reserve figure, the auctioneer will always seek instructions from the vendor during the auction before selling

- Revised auction reserve figure, again the auctioneer will seek instructions.

All or any of these figures can be changed in writing by the seller prior to the auction and on auction day by confirming a change on the auction reserve letter.

The sellers will be present at the auction and will take up a seat in the front bedroom. The auction will be held in the front garden so they can hear and see what is happening. Sometimes the sellers prefer to be at a neighbour's house and listen in on the action by phone. Sometimes the sellers mingle with the auction crowd, sometimes they stand with the auctioneer or lock themselves in an adjacent room.

When there are no more questions from the sellers, the set-the-scene meeting is completed and we all look forward to a positive outcome on auction day.

The following day is Friday, the day before auction, so the agent uses this opportunity to call all interested buyers and invite them to pre-register to bid and answer any questions they may have about the auction proceedings. We remind them that they will need to register to bid prior to the auction and they will need photo ID to do so. If they are the successful bidder, they are required to sign the unconditional contract on the spot and pay a 10% deposit (unless negotiated prior to going to auction). Most buyers either bring along their personal cheque book or obtain a blank counter cheque from their bank which they can complete on the day. Some buyers will bring a bank cheque for an amount which is 10%

of what they expect to pay. If they are the successful buyer on the day, this amount is accepted on signing with any shortfall topped up the following Monday.

STEP 2 – SOLD OR NEGOTIATED AT AUCTION

It's auction day and auction time is 9:30 am. The agent has put out their auction signage and the property is open for inspection at 9 am for any buyers to have another look. There are always new buyers inspecting who have not seen the home before. Some are neighbours, and some have no idea there is to be an auction today, while some are 'trusted advisers' of buyers who plan to bid.

The agent has a registration table set up and buyers who wish to register to bid line up to exchange their details for a registration number on an auction paddle. Lucky paddle number 8 has already been taken, so 88 is the next request. Four buyers have registered to bid. Two are buyers who have inspected during the campaign, two are new buyers who have only just viewed the home this morning.

The auctioneer arrives and greets the sellers and discusses strategy with them. Everyone is excited and nervous at the same time. The crowd of about 30 people gather in the front garden and the auctioneer gets underway at 9:30 am. The auction begins with the legal information the auctioneer is required to read out and a description of the property, and then the all-important call for an opening bid or offer. The silence is deafening; none of the potential bidders say anything, so the auctioneer makes a joke along the lines of, 'Did I mention how quiet this location is?'

The agent moves between the registered bidders to have a quiet word with them to encourage the buyers to make a bid while the auctioneer offers a figure to get the bidding started. Unfortunately, despite the agent's best efforts none of the registered bidders will make a bid. Although they are standing, we describe the buyers as 'sitting on their hands'.

After what seems like an eternity, the auctioneer still has no bids and seeks instructions from the sellers. The auctioneer places the 'seller's bid', clearly indicating it as the seller's bid. This bid is not the reserve price: this is a bid to encourage registered bidders to make their own bid. Even if there were only one registered bidder at the auction, that bidder is still competing with the seller to reach a figure where a deal may be done. If the buyer's bid is on the low side, then the seller's bid helps realign the expectation to encourage the buyer to increase their bid.

In this case, there are no further bids and the property is passed in on the seller's bid. As there were no bids from registered buyers, there is no buyer with the advantage of first to negotiate, so the auctioneer recommends all interested buyers now negotiate directly with the agent. The auction is concluded, and the crowd disperses. Many of the neighbours compare notes and voice their own opinion on what could or should have happened and who was to blame. Neighbours have a vested interest in a strong sale price for every home in their street, as it may be a reflection of the value of their property, so it is not surprising when one neighbour refers to the morning's proceedings as a 'failed auction'. Rarely have I met a neighbour who was happy with any sale price in their street.

The agent meets with each of the registered bidders to see what their level of interest is in the home. While they did register, they did not bid so are they now interested in negotiating to buy the home and at what price? The seller's bid is a starting point for negotiation. Of the two known bidders, one wishes to negotiate and the other walks away with no further interest. Of the two unknown bidders, both tell the agent they were hoping to pick up the property for less than the seller's bid and if the seller decides to sell for less, could the agent get back to them.

The agent sits down with the one buyer left to discuss an offer. This is the same buyer who made the pre-auction offer and then pulled out. He is more convinced than before that he could have paid too much prior to auction, as there doesn't seem to be any other buyer interest here at the auction. He wants to offer less than his pre-auction offer, and despite much discussion nothing else can be achieved today, so the buyer and the agent agree to talk again in the afternoon.

If the buyer comes back before midnight that day and an agreement can be made with the seller and contracts can be signed the same day and payment made, then the sale is still deemed to be sold at auction. If no deal is done the same day then the property converts to a private treaty sale, generally with a price set by the seller. In this case, despite agreeing to discuss his offer that afternoon, the buyer was out of reach for the rest of the day.

The following day is Sunday and the agent gets a call from a buyer who has inspected the property but did not register to bid at the auction. He attended the auction but was at the back of the crowd and did not step forward. He was waiting to see what happened at the auction and he is aware of the seller's bid and the new price that is now on the property. He is aware that the agent is talking to the other buyer. He is interested in the property and he makes an offer that is higher than the seller's bid but lower than the asking price.

The agent meets with the sellers face to face and discusses the options. He calls the buyer back who, with some encouragement, increases his offer on two accounts and the sellers agree to accept his offer. As the property is no longer under auction conditions, the agreement is not binding. However, the agent emails a sales advice document to both conveyancers so they can get the ball rolling first thing Monday morning. The agent leaves a message for the original potential buyer that there is new interest, however that buyer doesn't call back.

10. GETTING THE DEAL DONE

STEP 1 – SALES ADVICE AND TERMS

The sales advice allows both conveyancers to discuss the contract and agree or disagree to amendments to clauses and conditions. The seller has stated that they will only accept an unconditional exchange, as if at auction - that is, there will be no cooling off period.

The contract of sale was created by the seller's conveyancer. It's their document and the special clauses it contains were created by them. The buyer's conveyancer is presented with the seller's contract and conditions and it goes without saying that they will seek to vary something. It's very rare that a buyer's conveyancer won't request some change to the contract.

Many of the changes requested are standard requests. One side wants to vary the inclusions or exclusions, vary the settlement date, vary the release of deposit clause, vary the default interest rate in relation to a penalty or add or delete a clause regarding the condition or repair to a part of the property.

Some of these changes will directly relate to the building report or strata report for the property, which may highlight items or issues that may have a future estimated cost projection. For instance, there could be a strata special levy of $50,000 that is being paid in instalments and at the time of sale still has half the costs to be paid. The negotiation may be that the seller pays it all up to date at settlement or that the buyer takes over responsibility for the unpaid portion at settlement.

Many buyers' conveyancers seek to delete the clause that releases the deposit to the seller. However, the deposit release usually has conditions attached to the effect that the deposit can only be released for the purposes of being used as the deposit on another property the seller wishes to purchase. That is, the deposit is transferred from one real estate agent's trust account to another agent's trust account. The funds are not just given to the seller for them to spend on whatever they like.

The buyer has not yet seen the building and pest report, so they request that the agent forwards that to them. There are some concerns, and the buyer asks a builder friend to inspect the home that afternoon. The agent meets the builder and he inspects the property with the report in his hand. The builder friend identifies that to fix one of the concerns in the report could run to $20,000; the agent offers to call another builder around to give his own estimate.

The buyer will be looking to take the full amount off the purchase price while the seller will be looking to minimise their loss by having their own 'expert' estimate the repairs at less. In most cases it is a give-and-take negotiation, because neither party is looking for a 'deal breaker' just some acknowledgement that a problem exists and needs to be addressed. A sense of fair play from both sides is required to avoid derailing the deal due to inflated egos standing in the way of a reasonable outcome.

The agent and the buyer discuss the building concern and the agent in turn discusses it with the seller. The agent speaks with a builder about potential costs. The seller agrees to include a $5,000 allowance for the work to be carried out. The agent discusses this concession with the buyer who reluctantly agrees, and the sale price is set $5,000 lower, which is a big win for the seller who, because of the agent's expertise, is now $15,000 better off.

The paperwork is amended, and the seller meets the agent at their office to sign the final contract.

The buyer has an appointment the following day with their conveyancer to sign the contract. The buyer's 12 noon appointment is delayed and pushed back, however the contract is finally signed at their conveyancer's office at 3 pm. The bank cheque for 10% of the sale price is attached and the 66W waiving the cooling off period is signed and attached by the buyer's conveyancer.

In this instance, the agent is then called to collect the buyer's signed contract from the conveyancer's city office and deliver it to the seller's conveyancer in North Sydney. The agent drops everything and becomes a courier, delivering the contract just before 4 pm. The seller's conveyancer now has both signed counterpart copies of the contract, the deposit cheque and the 66W cooling off waiver. When they are ready and have instructions from both sides to exchange contracts, they effect exchange and date the contracts. The phone call to the agent that exchange has taken place comes through at 5:30 pm. The agent calls both buyers and sellers to congratulate them on their purchase and their sale.

STEP 2 – BANK VALUATION

The real estate agent's duties are not complete yet. In most cases, the buyer will have applied for a mortgage, so the bank will require a property valuation to complete their formal finance application.

Depending on the amount of money the buyer is borrowing, their bank will either do a valuation prior to exchange of contracts or after exchange of contracts. If the property does not meet valuation, there could be a shortfall. If the risk of a shortfall is high then the valuation will likely be completed before contracts are exchanged.

The real estate agent will be contacted by a valuation company hired by the bank lender to make a time to physically inspect and document the property. Depending on the value of the property, the valuers may undertake a short-form or a long-form valuation on behalf of the lender. The agent will need to meet the valuer at the property, where they will take photographs, measure rooms and record the condition of the property. They will then prepare an official valuation and, using their experience and local area comparative sales, they will value the property at that date. The bank then sets its lending criteria on the report findings of this valuation. The valuation provides a figure as to what the property could be resold for should the bank need to sell the property to recoup their loan. As such, a valuation is dated and is not valid for more than 90 days from the valuation date.

Sometimes, I hear a potential seller say, 'I have a bank valuation higher than your estimate' but when I ask to see it, many times they can't produce it and if they can, then the valuation is much older than 90 days, which means that it is no longer considered valid.

Often, prior to exchange, a bank will ask for the buyer's signed front page of the contract with the agreed price completed to process their client's loan application and move their client's status from a pre-approval to a formal approval. This means that the seller and the buyer have agreed in principle to the sum and terms, however the buyer is reluctant to move forward to exchange until they have written formal approval on their loan. Recently, this process - which should have taken no more than three days - stretched out to eighteen days, with the bank going through the buyer's financial statements with a fine-tooth comb. If contracts have not exchanged, then the property stays on the market and the agent is still actively showing and selling the home to any other buyer. While the buyer and seller have an agreement in principle, it's up to the buyer to make the next step to exchange, which they are uncomfortable doing if they are still waiting on the formal bank approval. It can be an anxious time for both parties waiting on a bank. It can also become more complicated when another buyer decides to make an offer on the property as well, particularly if they also require formal bank approval for their loan. The agent negotiates with all interested buyers and presents the facts to the seller, because whatever the offer and the terms, it's the seller's decision that is final.

If the buyer and the seller decide to go ahead and exchange contracts with the five-day cooling off period, to allow time for the formal bank approval, then the buyer does not put down the usual 10% deposit, they only put down 0.25% of the purchase price. So, if the purchase price is $500,000 then the holding deposit is only $1,250. This is another reason why I am not a fan of the cooling off period and much prefer the 66W waiver of the cooling off period.

STEP 3 – PHYSICAL SIGNING AND EXCHANGE OF CONTRACTS

Our contract of sale is a counterpart system. Although the front page of the contract of sale has space allocated for the seller to sign and the buyer to sign underneath, along with witness signatures to their right, the seller and the buyer do not sign the same contract of sale. There are two identical contracts of sale or counterparts.

Depending on the location and availability of the conveyancers on both sides, contracts are generally exchanged by the seller's conveyancer or with permission by the purchaser's conveyancer. Alternatively, with agreement by both sides, contracts can be exchanged by the real estate agent. While I have exchanged contracts in the past many times without incident, I believe the seller and the buyer should deal with their conveyancers in person. I feel confident that they have received the very best advice prior to signing the contract when this happens. It's important to remember that it is an official legal document and it should be respected as such.

The seller will generally make an appointment to attend their conveyancer's office so they can be talked through the physical pages of the contract, showed the clauses that have been added or deleted, asked to initial any changes to clauses to acknowledge they agree, and ask any questions they may have, including regarding the settlement period. Once the seller is comfortable that the contract represents their position, they will sign the front page of the contract on the line that says 'Vendor'. If there are two or more owners, then they will sign beside each other in that location. Across from the seller's signature is a space for the witness to the signature. I am told that it is not required for a witness to sign it; however, if a witness is present, it can't hurt to sign.

The seller's signed contract generally stays with the seller's conveyancer unless other arrangements have been made. Other arrangements may include the seller making an appointment with their real estate agent to sign the contract in their agent's presence instead of their conveyancer's. If their conveyancer is not available but has discussed the contract on the phone with their client, the seller may choose to sign the contract at the real estate agent's office or another location of their choice.

Depending on the availability and location of both conveyancers and the signing parties, the seller's conveyancer may have given written agreement and permission to the buyer's conveyancer for their side to effect exchange of contracts. The third option is that both sides give the real estate agent permission to effect exchange of contracts. In this case, the agent will hold the signed seller's contract and arrange for the buyer to attend their office to sign their counterpart contract.

Once the agent has both the vendor's and purchaser's signed contracts side by side in their office, they will check that the two counterparts are identical. This is done by physically comparing each contract page by page to check they are identical. In the event that a page is missing (sometimes there's been a photocopy machine issue) or a page requires a clause to be crossed out, the agent refers to the written instructions from the seller's conveyancer to ensure that all changes are made on both copies so that both counterparts are identical. One copy has been signed by the seller and the other by the buyer.

If the property is to be exchanged with a 66W waiving the five-business-day cooling off period then a copy of this page, issued and signed by the buyer's conveyancer, must also be included in the buyer's copy. Lastly, the receipt for deposit money transferred, or the bank cheque or counter cheque for the agreed deposit amount, should also be attached to the seller's contract. Once the agent has accounted for all documents, it is usual practice to call the seller's conveyancer to advise them that all documents are accounted for and ask for instructions to proceed with exchange. The seller's conveyancer may have already received instructions from the buyer's conveyancer to exchange or they may make a call to obtain permission, and once both conveyancers give the agent permission to proceed, the agent will physically exchange the two side by side contracts on the desk and exchange has been effected.

The seller's conveyancer will then instruct the agent to write in the date of contract, which becomes the effective exchanged date in relation to the settlement period. Photocopies of both front pages, the 66W and the cheque are then made and scanned and emailed to both conveyancers and filed in the real estate agent's folder. The counterparts are then delivered to the conveyancers for the other side; that is, the seller's conveyancer will receive the buyer's contract and the buyer's conveyancer will receive the seller's contract. Delivery may be done by the agent, by courier or express post.

In the case of an auction, the conveyancers are unlikely to be present, so the real estate agent has to be sure they have the latest edition of the contract of sale, which may have changed over the course of a four- or five-week campaign, supplied by the seller's conveyancer just prior to auction date. Some conveyancers will physically mail out two identical and original contracts to the real estate agent to be used as auction contracts. The agent will also ensure they have an email or cover letter giving them authority to exchange contracts at auction, which is often on a Saturday when, most likely, the seller's conveyancer will not be contactable.

Where buyers and sellers are physically out of town, contracts can still be exchanged by agreement using fax, email or docu-sign. The original front page of the contract with the original signatures will be required prior to settlement. However in most cases a faxed, emailed or docu-signed page will be acceptable. Some sellers are representing family and friends and are working under authority of a Power of Attorney. If this is the case, a copy of this document needs to be supplied to the conveyancer by the seller, and as the agent I would keep a copy in my files as well.

STEP 4 – PUTTING UP THE SOLD STICKER

All the agents in our office work as a team, so when someone has a sale exchange, we are all excited for them. There is a real sense of achievement when a property is unconditionally exchanged, particularly if it has been a challenging sale or it might have just sold for a record price. Whatever the circumstances of the sale, it deserves a SOLD sign on the signboard to tell the world. Sometimes the seller is the most emotional and is so excited by the result that they ask to help put the SOLD sticker up with me. As you can imagine, there are photos taken as the SOLD sticker is carefully applied to avoid bubbles, always in an upward direction from left to right, much like a tick of approval.

Sometimes the buyer is the one who wants to help put up the SOLD sticker and their kids all help make it a family affair. I always take photos for them so they can share them with family and friends.

The agent will also mark the property as sold online. Both realestate.com.au and domain.com.au websites prefer the agent to disclose the sold price and reward the agent with higher visibility for sold properties that display the sold price. However, sometimes a seller or a buyer requests that the sold price is not disclosed online. If this is the request, the agent can mark the property as 'sale price not disclosed' by ticking a box on the website.

The sale price is then not shown and is replaced by the words 'Contact agent'. The agent can expect phone calls from data marketing companies asking for the sale price so they can update their own records, and in turn the price will leak out to the websites and it may be displayed despite the 'do not display' instruction.

Additionally, when the property settles, the sold price is reported to the Valuer General and it becomes public knowledge and again, will be displayed online. The agent did all they could to protect the price but eventually it will get out. Often an excited seller or buyer will tell a friend or tell another agent and that's all it takes for the websites to find out what the property sold for. Once it is online, it is all but impossible to remove.

I really like our new company SOLD sticker, which has evolved from a round SOLD to a landscape-shaped sticker which says PROUDLY SOLD, because it is. I take a huge amount of pride in every sale and if neither buyer nor seller can be there as I put up the sticker, I take a photo and text it to them with the caption 'Winner of Photo of the Week', which always gets a smile.

STEP 5 – DEPOSIT MONEY – WHO, WHERE AND TFN

There are two types of sales: conditional (holding deposit) and unconditional (agreed percentage).

If the property exchange has been agreed to with a cooling off period of five business days, then the holding deposit for conditional exchange is 0.25% of the purchase price, with the agreed balance paid on expiration of the cooling off period. For example, if the purchase price is $1,000,000 then the holding deposit is $2,500 paid on exchange of contracts. The property is then deemed to be 'under offer' and it is no longer actively marketed. If the buyer decides not to go ahead, for any reason, then they forfeit the holding deposit amount to the seller and the property is available for sale again. If the buyer does proceed, then they need to pay the balance of the agreed deposit, which is usually 10%, by the expiration of the cooling off period.

If there is no cooling off period offered or agreed to, then the buyer must pay the full agreed deposit on exchange of contracts and supply the 66W waiver, forgoing the cooling off option. The usual deposit as specified on the contract of sale is 10%; however, it is not uncommon these days for buyers to wish to offer 5% on exchange. This is part of the negotiation and offer process. If the seller agrees to accept a 5% deposit, the front page of the contract of sale is not varied, but a clause relating to the deposit is inserted into the 'special conditions' as agreed.

If the buyer is unable to complete the unconditional contract of sale and settle on the agreed date, then the seller has the right to rescind the contract, if the contract allows, and the buyer forfeits their deposit in full - that is, 10% of the purchase price.

Here's an example. If the property price is $500,000, then the 10% deposit is $50,000 and this is forfeited if the contract is not completed. This deposit amount is held in the agent's trust account, so it is easily transferred to the seller, less the agent's fee. Although in this instance the sale did not proceed, the agent has done their job to secure a buyer and exchange contracts; it is the buyer who has not performed.

In the instance that the seller accepted a lesser deposit, say 5%, and the buyer paid that amount, say $25,000 on exchange, and they don't settle the contract, then the buyer is still legally bound to pay the outstanding 5% deposit. However, as there is only 5% in the agent's trust account, and the buyer may have financial reasons why they couldn't proceed, it will become a legal battle for the seller to get their outstanding monies.

On a higher priced sale, say a $5 million sale, where the 10% deposit amounts to half a million dollars ($500,000) some buyers will want to offer the 5%, as they may only have $250,000 that is not invested in some other account. It's the seller's decision as to whether they accept the lower deposit amount, as they bear the risk. When a buyer is seeking a 5% deposit and an extended settlement, alarm bells should ring, as the risk is amplified over time.

When the agent opens a new account within their trust account for the deposit on your property, they also require a tax file number (TFN) to show that the depositor is an Australian citizen. Otherwise the bank will charge 50% withholding tax on any interest earned in the account during the settlement period. While the interest may be small, it's easy to avoid this impost by supplying your tax file number.

The seller's conveyancer can also nominate that the deposit paid for the property be held in their conveyancer's trust account instead of the real estate agent's trust account.

If agreed to by the seller, then the deposit may also be paid by way of a Deposit Bond, which is essentially a bank-guaranteed bond for the amount required, offered as surety in place of cash.

11. SETTLEMENT

STEP 1 – BUYER'S REMORSE

After all the excitement of unconditional exchange has passed, the reality of the purchase sets in. In some cases, there may be buyer's remorse, where the buyer has been influenced by friends and family saying perhaps they paid too much or there was another property which suited them better that they should have bought. Sometimes, it's just the exhaustion of finally having purchased that is almost an anti-climax, rather than specific buyer's remorse.

Equally, there may be some seller's remorse. Have we done the right thing? Was there a buyer who would have paid more? Did we get the best possible price for our property? In almost every case I have been involved in, the seller feels a great sense of relief and accomplishment after unconditional exchange. They move from uncertainty to certainty, with the understanding that they are now moving on with their lives. Often, they are grateful for that one buyer who was prepared to pay more than anyone else to buy their home. They acknowledge they are in a fortunate position.

STEP 2 – BUYER ACCESS PRIOR TO SETTLEMENT

Between exchange and settlement, the buyer will be preparing to move into their new home. This often means they need to decide what they will bring with them and what they will leave behind, especially if they are downsizing. I am often asked by the buyer if I can arrange another inspection of the property 'to measure up' to see where their furniture will go. As the agent, I am the middleman between the buyer and the seller during the 'no-man's land' period of settlement. The buyer is asking to inspect again with an expectation of hearing, 'Absolutely, no problem', while the seller is turning their own life upside down to move out of the property on time.

Remember that the last time the buyer saw the home it was 'brochure ready', potentially styled by experts to look amazing with not a thing out of place. Now that same buyer wants to inspect the property again when it looks like a bomb went off. There may be half-packed moving boxes, missing pieces of furniture, plates in the sink, the garden will be neglected - it's the opposite image to what the buyer has in their head of the wonderful home they have purchased.

It's no wonder many sellers say, 'Sorry, but no, it's not convenient', because it simply isn't. They have already put their life on hold during the sales campaign and now they are moving, so the house is a real mess. The seller doesn't want the buyer to see the house in such a mess. The buyer expects a mess and is simply hoping to 'measure up'.

Often I hear, 'Tell the buyer to get their measurements from the floorplan' after a request to inspect. As the man in the middle, I can understand both sides holding their ground, but the reality is that the home still belongs to the seller, and if they are not comfortable allowing the buyer back in while the home is in disarray, then it is their decision, not mine and certainly not the buyer's. It is also not a contractual requirement. If anything, it's a courtesy that may or may not be extended.

The same goes for buyers who want to bring their trades and decorators through, to get quotes and orders underway ahead of the settlement date. If the property is vacant, and the sellers agree, sure, I can help make that happen, but under no circumstances can the tradespeople start work before settlement. It's the seller's decision and that decision may be 'No'. Importantly, even if the property is vacant, buyers are not permitted to occupy or begin work of any type without express written permission from the seller's conveyancer. Until settlement is complete, the property is still owned and maintained by the seller.

The seller also needs to continue to insure the building in case a natural or even a man-made disaster occurs. Remember the Sydney super-storms on 28th November 2018? TV hosts called it 'Stormaggeddon'. These storm cells brought down trees on homes and flooded hundreds of properties. Imagine you had exchanged but not settled and your future home was decimated by floodwater or the neighbour's tree came down over your future roof. You would be looking to the current owner for insurance protection and to make good. The seller is still responsible for their home until the keys are handed over. So, don't even ask if you can get in early to paint and polish the floorboards when you don't own the home yet.

STEP 3 – THE SELLER IS PACKING TO MOVE

From exchange to settlement is an agreed number of days: the default period on the contract is 42 days or six weeks. Packing to move from a property can be overwhelming and, if this is the case, I will help you by recommending people I know who specialise in helping other people move. The first decision is, where are you moving to and what will you take with you? If you are downsizing, then the contents of a four-bedroom family home will not physically fit in a two-bedroom apartment, so you need to consider what belongings you will move with you and what you need to let go of.

Letting go can be an emotional time, especially if you are the custodian of your parent's dining table that has been in the family for years but just won't fit in the new home. Some buyers are so attached to a piece of furniture that they struggle to part with it and may even use it as a reason why they can't downsize. It's also hard to find buyers for old-world, dark, timber ten-seat dining tables with ornate carved chairs and velvet inserts. Once upon a time, these items cost thousands of dollars, however now you will struggle to even give them away. It's a dilemma that leaves some people emotionally lost.

The contract specifies the inclusions and exclusions, but not everything is itemised, so what are the grey areas? If you have a five-year-old, wall-mounted TV on a universal bracket with concealed cabling, should you take it or leave it? You can probably replace the TV with one that is twice as good for half as much as you paid, and when you remove the bracket from the wall you will have to get a painter to repair the wall and repaint, so why not leave it for the new owner? Don't forget to leave the remote as well!

Pots and urns on the balcony or terrace are often a challenge to move and many removalists will not remove them, citing health and safety issues because of their size and weight. So check if your buyer is happy to keep the pots or if they may have to be broken up to be removed safely.

The other question is regarding the clothes dryer bracket. Some apartments include the wall-mounted dryer as an inclusion, but if you do take the dryer down, also take the bracket with you, as the buyer will likely do the same with their bracket.

Many properties have cans of paint, spare tiles, carpet and floorboards left over from renovations and most buyers are happy to have them left behind. Occasionally, a buyer wants them all cleared away. If this has not been discussed beforehand, it becomes the agent's problem to get rid of them at the last minute.

One way or another, the property needs to be vacant in time for a final inspection prior to settlement. Decisions need to be made and removalists called. You can, of course, simply put off the decision-making to another time, and many people do this. They instruct the removalists to take only selected items to their new address and to pack and store the remainder. If you can't decide what to do then storage is an option, although over time it can be an expensive one. If you can decide, then divide your belongings up into four groups: keep, sell, donate or throw out.

Once things go into storage, they often stay there, and the monthly storage fees mount up. Years later, the value of the contents of the storage garage won't even cover the storage costs to date, so before you store things, think twice about what you will do with them and when, and you may save time and money avoiding storage altogether.

STEP 4 – PROFESSIONAL CLEANERS AND PRESENTATION

You can tell a lot about people by the way they decide to leave their property. The buyer is entitled to a final inspection of the property prior to settlement for the purposes of confirming that the previous owner or occupier has now vacated the property and it is 'vacant possession'. The final inspection is done prior to settlement: sometimes the morning of, sometimes the day before, depending on availability. If the seller has purchased and arranged for a simultaneous exchange, then they are likely to still be living in the property right up until settlement day, which makes it almost impossible to carry out a final inspection.

Whether the sellers are doing a simultaneous settlement, or they have moved out a few days ago, I like to think that they will leave the property in the same state or better than they would like to find it themselves. Unfortunately, it's up to the seller to leave the property as they feel fit and not all sellers do the right thing.

However, it's worth noting that the contract does not specify in what condition the property is required to be left, just that it must be 'vacant possession'. That means the seller can effectively leave the packing to the removalists and simply walk out without any further responsibility, and some do. I always attend the final inspection with the buyer and sometimes we are both shocked and horrified at the condition the property has been left in. You can only imagine.

It's frustrating and disappointing for both the buyer and myself. It means that all our prior discussions about leaving the home in a fit and proper state have been ignored. Several times I have had to call our professional cleaner team (at my expense) to come and spend several hours bringing the property up to scratch. Sometimes buyers threaten not to settle unless the property is professionally cleaned, but leaving the property clean and tidy is not a contractual requirement.

More often than not, however, sellers heed my recommendations about the moving process. We know it's a huge day, tempers flare, things go wrong, sometimes it rains, things get broken, and once the property is empty of all furniture and belongings you really get the first sense of just how much cleaning it really needs. That's why we recommend professional cleaners to come in and take over the systematic cleaning of the property from top to bottom. It may be the first full professional vacuum and clean the property has had in 20 years.

It's often been six weeks since the buyer last saw the property, which is when it was 'photo ready' in the middle of the sales campaign. It's worth remembering to have the gardener mow the lawn and sweep the paths and even clean the windows, so that the buyer remains excited about their purchase just as they were the day on which they signed the contract.

STEP 5 – FINAL INSPECTION

Buyers are entitled to a 'final inspection' prior to settlement. It's important to be clear what this inspection is for. It is simply to check that the seller has vacated and left the property in a reasonable condition, as it was last time they saw it during the sales campaign. Importantly, there is nothing in the contract of sale that sets out any guidelines as to what condition the seller must leave the property. It's entirely up to the vacating seller. There is a reasonable expectation that it should be left in the condition that you would expect to find it if you were the buyer. Again, this is only what a reasonable person would do and sometimes people surprise me and all reason goes out the door with them!

I have been left with properties that have not met my expectations on more than one occasion. I was told it was no reflection on me as their agent, it's just that they ran out of time to have the property cleaned, so it is what it is. That doesn't sit well with me. Although the seller is my current client, the buyer will be my new client. As the person in the middle, I do my best to ensure I don't offend either party, but I do like to ensure that both parties are aware of what I expect of them.

Ideally, I recommend that final inspection is conducted a minimum of 24 hours before settlement, that the seller has completed their pack and move, they have completely vacated and the professional cleaners have started if not finished their full property clean. It's not a final inspection to check that the seller has vacated, if they still have possessions in the property. If they are still there and they still have their belongings in the property, then they have not vacated. Technically speaking, the seller has until one second before settlement to vacate but practically speaking that's stretching the friendship beyond anything reasonable, so let's look at a best-practice scenario instead.

I always recommend that if settlement is booked in for Friday at 12 noon that the seller be completely vacated by 12 noon on Thursday, a full 24 hours ahead - not the morning of settlement.

As the seller, why not spoil yourself knowing that all your furniture and belongings are safely packed up in a container or truck? You can go and stay one night in a five-star hotel and enjoy a break from the ordinary - after all, you deserve it! This allows for a professional cleaner to arrive at 12:30 and work through the afternoon to present the home as clean as possible. The final inspection can be booked for, say, 5 pm the day before settlement, when the home is both vacant and clean. The inspection will then simply be a cursory check to see that the property has been vacated. In the unlikely event that the removalists have damaged a wall or a doorway, or caused a problem that requires fixing, it can be agreed on with time on your side, not left as a scramble for compensation at the last minute. If it has rained all moving day, it will take longer to move your things and the removalists will have walked their wet boots throughout the house. This will take longer to clean and isn't acceptable to just say, 'Not my problem'.

It is unreasonable to expect to be able to sleep in the house on the Thursday night, then have the removalists be on time at 7 am to have you all packed and out by 10 am, to then allow cleaners to do their best work in under two hours without allowing for the final inspection.

Buyer introduction

After negotiation, your real estate agent is the go-between for your sale and rarely do the buyer and the seller meet. This is mainly because the real estate agent does all the running around. However, no one knows the daily ins and outs of your home like you do, so sometimes it makes sense for the seller to meet the buyer at the home for a quick tour to answer any questions. I always provide a handover checklist for the buyer with questions answered by the seller about the home.

This list includes information about the keys, the council, garbage collection, remote controls, tradespeople who are familiar with the property, alarm systems and even neighbours and best restaurants in walking distance.

Essentially, I am trying to answer every question before it gets asked.

STEP 6 – CONVEYANCER DETAILS PRIOR TO SETTLEMENT

The seller and the buyer each have a conveyancer looking after the settlement of the property for them. Prior to settlement, some housekeeping is required. With about seven days to go, the seller's conveyancer will check details with the seller such as:

- settlement money and rates notices
- final inspection
- handover of keys at settlement
- change of name for service providers.

At settlement, the seller's council rates, water rates and strata levies (if applicable) are adjusted on a pro-rata basis to the settlement date. Their conveyancer will need the latest copy of council, water and strata levy (if applicable) notices. Closer to the settlement date, the conveyancer will be provided with a payout figure for any mortgage or loan that the seller has outstanding. Any surplus funds will be banked into their account after settlement. The agent will deduct their commission and costs from the deposit they hold and then transfer the balance of the money into the account the seller has nominated.

As discussed earlier, under the contract the purchaser is entitled to a final inspection of the property which they will arrange with the real estate agent, and this is ideally done either the day before or (not ideally) on the morning of settlement.

Once settlement has taken place, the purchaser is entitled to collect the keys from the real estate agent and take possession of the property.

The change of name and address for the buyer for council, water, and strata bills is part of the settlement process. The seller will need to arrange for the cancellation or transfer of telephone, electricity, gas, internet, Foxtel and any other services they have.

STEP 7 – SETTLEMENT DAY

In the past, we have relied on manual settlement of property transactions by a nominated settlement agent who physically had to manage all the documents in a physical property file to effect settlement.

From the 1st July 2019, all conveyancers will only be able to use the electronic settlement process called PEXA (Property Exchange Australia), Australia's online property exchange network. PEXA was established to speed up and streamline the property settlement process for conveyancers and financial institutions to lodge documents with the Land Registries and complete financial settlements electronically, all around the country.

This e-conveyancing provides greater certainty and a faster and easier transaction, so the sale proceeds are processed as cleared funds to the nominated accounts. From a real estate agent's perspective, we are excited by e-conveyancing and welcome this change for the better.

STEP 8 – ORDER ON THE AGENT

Settlement is booked in by the conveyancers in advance, so your settlement will be allocated a time to happen so that all the paperwork can be ready and in place. Electronic settlement has streamlined the manual tasks; however, we still need to follow due process. For the agent, that includes waiting for the conveyancer to issue The Order on the Agent. This amounts to the conveyancer's instructions that the matter has now officially been finalised and calls on the agent to account for the deposit money and expenses to the seller and gives us permission to release the keys to the buyer.

During the sales campaign, I only have the keys I need to access the property. It's usually the spare key, as the owners are still using their regular keys and remotes. On settlement, I always put the keys I have on our own special key ring and package them in a special presentation box to give the 'handing over of the keys' a little bit of pomp and ceremony as befits the occasion. This may be the first time the new owner has ever purchased a property and I'd like to think we have presented the keys in a memorable fashion. Of course, a memorable gift accompanies the keys: after all, this new buyer may one day become our next seller, so it's important that they feel we went over and above their expectations.

Many new owners wish to meet at our office to collect the keys while others ask me to meet them at the property, which I am happy to do. I always ask the seller to leave all the spare keys and remotes in the kitchen drawer - that way they can't get packed by the removalists, which has happened many times before. It's always appreciated when the seller has left any manuals or appliance instructions in the drawer as well. Often relatives have a spare key so, if they can't all be back in the property by settlement, ask the relatives to pop them in an envelope and leave them in the letterbox.

The Order on the Agent may also contain account details and payment amounts for specific transfers of the funds in the trust account. The conveyancer may instruct the agent to pay funds into different accounts to finalise outstanding matters in a timely manner.

The deposit amount is usually deposited in the real estate agent's trust account and invested in a 30-day term deposit account prior to settlement. A separate account is opened for each property transaction and any interest earned is split between the seller and the buyer equally - unless otherwise agreed.

The agent's success fee is deducted, along with any outstanding marketing costs, from the deposit amount and on settlement the balance is transferred to the nominated accounts.

STEP 9 – AGENT'S REVIEW REQUEST

Online real estate agent reviews are the new equivalent of a written testimonial, which only used to happen when the buyer or the seller was so completely delighted with the agent and the service provided that they took the trouble to hand-write a thank-you card in appreciation.

These days it is all about agent reviews online, because potential sellers can check the reviews on a potential agent to get some feeling for how well they are doing their job. Of course, selling real estate is more to me than just doing my job. If it ever just became a job, I would give it up. It is a lifestyle and one I very much appreciate, because I am lucky enough to be part of a life-changing experience for both the seller and the buyer and their families.

Online reviews are an introduction to the agent. To find out more, you need to go to the next step and give them a call. You don't have to be selling this month to start to interview agents for the future task of selling your home. Every week I will meet a potential client at the coffee shop across from our office, just to get the conversation started. As you can now appreciate, there are many steps on your Journey to Sold, and calling your agent for a chat is the most important one.

12. HOME AGAIN

STEP 1 – THE END OF YOUR JOURNEY

Thank you for travelling with me as your tour guide on your Journey to Sold. I hope you have gained a valuable insight into the process of selling your home, and that this book becomes a resource for you that helps you on your own journey, when the time is right for you.

My sales process is constantly evolving as technology changes and I find new ways to improve my productivity and efficiency. I would like to invite you to register at my website www.journeytosold.com.au to receive additional resources and templates that will help you down the track.

Selling real estate is an extraordinary opportunity and I am humbled every time a seller chooses to put the keys of their home in my hand to represent their sale for them. I will never take that trust for granted and will always strive to improve and to deliver the most rewarding experience for my clients.

No matter how long you have been travelling - a day, a week, a month or longer - nothing ever feels as good as arriving home again. It's always good to be home.

13. DETOURS

STEP 1 – TRAVEL TIPS

This is a list of things you can do to sell your home faster. If you don't see yourself having the time to do this, then call professional help. It still needs to be done. How you show your home says a lot about how you have cared for your home over the years. You want buyers to connect with your home.

Do a walk-through. Start at the front gate with a pen and paper and walk from the front of the house to the back, and write down anything that takes your eye for the wrong reason. That will give you a buyer's perspective on the condition of your property.

Declutter. We have all heard the word 'declutter', but what does it really mean? In a nutshell, it means getting rid of one-third of everything: give it away, sell it or throw it away.

Of the two-thirds that are left, store one-third off site, don't just move it to your garage. That leaves about one-third of your belongings that you use on a regular, day-to-day basis, and that's all you need to sell your home.

De-personalise. Get rid of family photos and things of great interest or value. Don't distract buyers with your possessions, keep things neutral so they can see themselves living in your home, not you.

Clear benchtops. If you still have stuff left on benchtops, clear it away. Clear tops of bedside tables, take magazines off coffee tables and water glasses out of bedrooms, clear tops of dressers, get rid of rubbish bins, phone chargers, medicine bottles, anything and everything - clear all the surfaces. Clear the fridge of advertising magnets and kids' artwork. Remove the energy-efficient stickers on appliances.

Clean. Now that most of your items are gone, let's give the house a thorough deep-clean - the type of clean it hasn't had for ages. Wipe out the shelves and cupboards. Really clean the bathrooms, really clean the kitchen and make it so that it is a spotless home that will even impress you!

Forgotten repairs. Stop living with those broken items and fix them today. If you have missing door handles, leaky taps, doors that don't close, anything that you know should be fixed but you never got around to it, now is the time to fix it.

Curtains and blinds. Pull up all your blinds and pull back the curtains. If they are broken, then remove them and replace them with off-the-shelf inexpensive alternatives. Clean the windows, because light makes buyers happy and happy buyers will pay more for your home.

Lightbulbs. Replace all your eco-friendly, low-wattage lightbulbs - particularly those curly-looking ones - with new bright-as-you-can-buy lightbulbs, preferably warm white 70-watt halogens (available in screw thread or bayonet). Suddenly you will see what buyers will see and that is an open, larger looking room.

Touch-ups. Now you can see your walls, cupboards and door frames. If they need paint touch-ups, get them painted. Check your sinks, showers and bath, and if they need re-caulking, get it done.

Neutral tones. If you have bright-coloured feature walls or bedrooms, paint them neutral tones. Soft white is ideal. Add colour with cushions and accessories.

Day spa experience. Invest in new, fluffy, white towels for the bathrooms and new bedlinen. Make your home feel like a day spa experience. It's not about how you live anymore, it's about selling the feeling of luxury. Make all the beds and add throws and extra pillows to make spaces more inviting. Keep the toilet lid closed.

Entrance. Buyers will line up at your front door to meet the agent, so make the area as inviting as possible. Hide your keys, coats and shoes, then keep it clean. Wipe down or paint the front door as well.

Street appeal. If you pull up in your car outside, how does your house look? How would you rate its street appeal? Mow and trim the lawns, remove dead shrubs from the garden, cut back foliage from the windows and the house, pressure-wash the paths and maybe even wash the house. Get rid of spider webs, particularly near the entrance.

Pets or no pets. While I am a fan of cats and dogs in their own home, when you are selling, the ideal selling space does not function well with dog food bowls, cat litter trays and fur around the house. Many buyers are just not tolerant of our furry friends and some are even allergic, so it's best to minimise their presence or send them on an early holiday during the sales campaign. That way you are set for those last-minute inspections which are sure to happen.

The day before open home day. Put the garbage out and use an essential oil diffuser to remove lingering smells. Candles can cause a fire if forgotten, so avoid them for safety's sake. Nothing beats fresh flowers in the kitchen and dining/ lounge area, so arrange some tastefully. Café music playing at a low volume in the lounge area will make your home more friendly. Consider showing your home on open home day as a special occasion and a bit of extra effort will reap rewards. A full renovation is likely to be very costly and may not earn you as much money as these smaller, targeted projects which, when all done together, will impress any buyer.

STEP 2 – GREEN IS GOOD

Does your home offer green credentials? Buyers are more and more in tune with eco-friendly products and your home is no different. You may think along the same lines, so be sure to let your agent know that your home offers green features such as concealed water tanks to water your vegetable patch and herb garden. You may have a composter or even a chook or two.

You may have roof-mounted solar panels which power parts of your home and feed excess energy back into the grid, lowering your overall power bill. You may have motion-detector lighting and infrared cameras that are connected to a hard-drive recorder and can be seen on your phone as part of your back-to-base alarm system.

Even recycling bins are worth mentioning, or an EV charger for an electric car: these are all features that make a home more attractive to different buyers. Some buyers value green credentials over views, others value privacy or peace and quiet, and many value pet-friendliness more than anything else.

STEP 3 – BUY AND SELL ASSESSMENT

Some sellers do an online search of their own address and find property websites that offer them an instant estimate of value. Often the range is very broad, making the estimates ridiculous at best. It's worth noting that the computer has never been to your house and, without a physical inspection, the data is at best a guess, not a valuation.

If all properties were the same, pricing them would be easy, but that's just not the case. When you are selling a property, you may have lived there for many years and just accept things at face value. There are things you no longer notice which may affect a buyer's position on value but don't concern you. Let's just look at a one-bedroom unit from a buyer's perspective to understand how they will determine the value of the apartment when comparing it with another one-bedroom unit. Obviously, a house will have even more to consider, but you may be surprised at the variables for a basic unit.

Size. What is the size of your apartment? This piece of information is easily found on the strata plan and depending on the age of the apartment will be written in square feet or square metres - and if it's in square feet there will be a conversion chart attached. Is the property under 50 sqm? This is important, because not all banks will provide finance for a property under 50 sqm. If you are selling a unit under this threshold, it's worth checking with a finance broker as to which banks are currently lending on this size apartment. If a buyer needs finance, they will need to deal with one of these banks or pay cash. Some banks will finance one-bedroom properties to a minimum of 40 sqm and some as small as 35 sqm; however, this does not include properties under management. Some banks will not finance studio apartments that do not have a full separate bedroom, while others require an internal laundry to be eligible for finance. Bank lending criteria changes so be sure to check the current position with your trusted broker.

Age. The age of your apartment is a factor, as is the condition of both the apartment and the building. Many buyers prefer new or near-new units over older buildings, as they may require less maintenance and already conform with all current legislation. I recently sold a one-bedroom unit in a 1960s building which included a $21,000 special levy per unit to update balconies to current standards.

Style. While Art Deco–style apartments are older, they are often favoured over later built units because they offer higher ceilings and a generous room size, but not all Art Deco apartments have balconies or car parking. Some buyers simply don't like the look of textured red-brick or blonde-brick buildings; some don't like the old feel or the old look of a property that hasn't kept up with the times.

Number of units. Is the apartment one of two units in a duplex, one of four in a two-storey building, one of ten in a three-storey building or one of 60 in a 16-storey building? Buyers generally favour a smaller, older building for peace and quiet or a newer, taller building that offers a district view.

Condition. When was the apartment last updated internally? Does it have an original kitchen and bathroom which are showing their age, or have they been updated in recent times? Buyers factor the cost of renovating into their offer price when they see missing tiles and old shower curtains.

Balcony. Many buyers insist on a property with a balcony off the living room; others also want a balcony off the bedroom for air flow and that 'open' feeling. Most also want a useable balcony they can put a table and chair on to be able to eat 'alfresco'. Not all buildings allow a barbecue anymore, but many buyers have entertaining in mind when they see a small balcony. Is the balcony covered or is it fully exposed to the sun all year round? Is the balcony facing another balcony next door, so that privacy is compromised?

Garden/terrace/rooftop. What's better than a balcony? Some buyers prefer a garden or terrace area which they can potter around in. Small gardens are favoured by downsizers who have just given up a large garden but still yearn for a small garden. Is the garden on the apartment title, or is it exclusive use through a by-law or is it shared common property that anyone can access?

Painting. When was the property last painted? Is the ceiling peeling? Are there strong-coloured feature walls that should be painted neutral?

Ceiling. Is the ceiling a popcorn ceiling, made from vermiculite that needs attention, with dated track lighting or cheap oyster-style lights? Has the unit been updated, with a flat gyprock ceiling installed to offer a 'shadowline' finish, and does it now have recessed LED lighting installed, without sacrificing overall height in the room?

Walls. Are they internal feature brick, cement render or gyprock finish? Do they need attention, paint or render?

Windows. Are there see-through blinds on the windows, block-out blinds or curtains? Are there plantation shutters or something to provide privacy at night? Are there any window coverings at all?

Floors. Is there carpet, and is it clean enough that you would be happy to lie down on it? Is there lino in the kitchen or does the apartment have timber-style floorboards throughout? Is the balcony a painted concrete surface or does it have a covering such as removeable timber slat squares to make it more attractive?

Air flow. Do the windows open or are they sealed up? Do you have double-glazed windows and can they be opened? Is there a ceiling fan, gas bayonet outlet or approved air conditioner to heat and cool the space to make it more comfortable?

Kitchen. Is the kitchen original, or has it had updates? What type of benchtops do you have? Is there a dishwasher? Is there an oven with a separate cooktop and ducted rangehood, or just a recirculating rangehood? Can you fit a full-size fridge in the space or is it too small? Is there gas cooking or electric? Are there sufficient cupboards and drawers or a pantry for storage?

Dining. Is there room for a stand-alone dining table, or is there a breakfast bar or somewhere to eat? Or is there not enough space for a table at all?

Study nook. Is there a place to work from a laptop that isn't the dining room table?

TV cabling. Is the TV/Foxtel cabling in the right place or do you need to run cables across the floor to have the TV where you want it? Is there a TV bracket mounted on the wall?

Storage. Is there a broom cupboard or place to keep a vacuum cleaner? Is there a linen press for storage? Does the bedroom have a built-in wardrobe and, if so, is it fitted with both hanging space and drawers?

Bathroom. Is the bathroom entrance separate from the bedroom, so that guests don't have to walk into the bedroom to access the ensuite? Is there a separate shower or is it a shower over the bath? Is there a cupboard in the bathroom or storage area for items?

Laundry. Is there an internal laundry with plumbing for a washing machine and a mount for a dryer and a tub with running water? Is there space for an internal clothesline? Is there a shared laundry room on each floor for specific units with allocated power points and supplied washers and dryers, or is it coin-operated supplied machines, or just a space to leave your own machines on a first-come first-served basis. Is there one laundry room on the ground floor and are there any clotheslines in the sunshine or undercover hanging areas?

Garbage room. Does the building have garbage chutes on each floor or a common bin area that is not close to your balcony or front door? Is it easily accessed? Who puts the bins out each week?

Outlook. What can you see when you look out of the living room and bedroom windows? Can the neighbours look back in? Is there an outlook of trees, the street, a laneway, the main road, a water view or a park?

Aspect. Does the balcony face north or north-east? Will the apartment get any direct sun at all in winter and, in summer, is there any protection from the sun such as an extendable awning? What is the apartment's position in the block relative to the surrounding buildings?

Access. Is there level access from the carpark or the street? Are there multiple storeys of stairs? Is it a third-storey walk-up or is there an elevator that services all floors including garage area? Is the elevator new or does it feel old and clunky? Is there just one elevator for the whole building, and if so, what would it mean if the elevator wasn't working for a few days?

Security. Does the building have a lockable front door and residents are responsible to keep it locked? Is there an audio or video intercom with door release for visitors? Does it remote-release the door to the garage and is there visitors' parking on site? Is the elevator unrestricted or do you need an owner's fob to access individual floors and common areas other than the fire exits? Is there a closed-circuit TV system and/or an on-site concierge or manager either full time or part time?

Location. Is the apartment on a main road with a main road address, at the front or at the back of the building, on the top floor, middle floor, ground floor? Is it facing north, south, east or west, with a larger building in your line of sight, a rooftop, a neighbour's balcony, neighbour's window, overlooking a car park, a children's park? Is it next door to a childcare centre, a bowling club or function centre that operates at night, or above a retail shop, a food shop, petrol station, hotel, building driveway, or adjacent to a bin collection area? Is the property conveniently located near facilities so that it has a high walkability score? Or do you need to drive to local attractions?

Facilities. Is the building older style with no internal facilities or is it a more modern building offering an indoor swimming pool, gymnasium, concierge, café, or rooftop barbecue and viewing area? Are there large common area gardens, double security parking and storage cages?

Strata report. Building facilities come with a cost, so buyers are mindful of the ongoing strata fees they will pay to own in a building. Find out the quarterly strata fees and how much money is in the administration and building works fund to ensure a strategic maintenance plan is in place to avoid the need for a special levy in the future.

Does the strata manager have a good relationship with the strata committee and do they have a solid ten-year plan in place, with a history of making the right decisions in relationship to the building maintenance? What is the ratio of owner-occupiers to tenants and are the strata fees in credit or arrears? Do the building residents enjoy an overall harmonious co-existence or is there pending litigation or ongoing disputes? Are the fire ordinances up to date and are there any registered complaints, outstanding payments, re-zoning discussions or outstanding matters which are never resolved at annual general meetings?

* * *

As you can appreciate, there are many variables that a buyer will consider, and different buyers will value different things at a different price. Sales of other property in the same building offer some starting point but only when an agent has assessed the property in person can they provide a reasonable estimate of selling price that you can rely on.

Sellers start out emotionally charged and buyers start out thinking logically. The logical price will attract buyers to inspect, the buyers will determine the market price and the agent will trigger the emotional buyer to pay a premium price. The process does not work in reverse. If you overprice the property at the start, then that may be the end of your journey. The buyer and the agent and the seller need to take the sales journey together to create and achieve the emotional price.

STEP 4 – WHAT COULD POSSIBLY GO WRONG?

We all hope for a problem-free sale, but sometimes things can go wrong that we can't anticipate and we just have to do the best we can. Here are some things that have happened to me during sales campaigns:

- Storm damage to the roof of the house such that it leaks
- The washing machine floods the floors, or the unit above floods the unit below
- The air conditioner breaks down on the hottest day of the year
- The power fails during the open home, so there is no lighting
- The elevator in the building stops working during the open home and is stuck
- The neighbour comes into the open home and complains about the owners out loud
- The fire alarm goes off in the building and the building is evacuated during an open home
- The seller passes away during the campaign, it then becomes an estate sale after probate

- The seller's dog bites a potential buyer at an open home; he turns out to be a lawyer
- A neighbour has vomited on the stairs outside the apartment I am selling just prior to open.

STEP 5 – TELL-TALE SIGNS

Here are ten tell-tale signs that a buyer is interested in buying your property:

1. They enquire online, asking the agent specific questions.
2. The attend an open home, ask questions and open cupboards and drawers.
3. They send a friend along to inspect for a second opinion.
4. They request the Contract of Sale and strata or building report.
5. They have a second inspection and bring along a family member.
6. They contact their finance broker/bank about the property.
7. They have their conveyancer review the contract and request changes.
8. They discuss price and other buyers' level of interest with the agent, possibly making an offer.
9. They confirm they will attend the auction and register to bid or pre-register.

10. They register at the auction and actively bid to secure the property.

STEP 6 – COMMUNITY

Real estate agents are often key supporters of their local community, and I applaud every agent who is helping clubs and organisations within the community without the expectation of getting something in return. For years I have sponsored the local croquet club, the bowling club, the junior hockey club and sea scouts, plus many one-off events and causes.

I also donate a backpack bed to the homeless every time I appraise or sell a property. I have donated over 250 backpack beds now through www.backpackbeds.org/au, and encourage you to consider donating to this worthy cause as well.

At the time of writing this book, I am about to sleep rough for the fifth year in a row on one of the coldest nights of the year to raise funds for the Vinnies CEO Sleepout® (www.ceosleepout.com.au). I have managed to raise over $25,000 for this very worthy cause.

I have also recently joined the ranks of the Change | Agent Initiative (www.mychangeagent.com.au). This is an organisation created to encourage real estate agents to support worthy projects in their community. You can find out more at my website, at www.geoffgrist.com.au/change-agent.

ALSO BY GEOFF GRIST

Sold Above Market is available from **www.soldabovemarket.com.au** - download an e-copy with our compliments.

Printed copies are available for purchase from **www.majorstreet.com.au**.

GLOSSARY OF TERMS

Apartment. A room or suite of rooms designed as a residence and generally located in a building occupied by more than one household.

Appraisal. An opinion of the potential rental or sale price of a property.

Body corporate. See *owners' corporation.*

Conveyancer. In law, conveyancing is the transfer of legal title of real property from one person to another, or the granting of an encumbrance such as a mortgage. It is a legal requirement in all jurisdictions that contracts for the sale of land be in writing.

Cooling off period. A set number of days after you have signed a contract of sale to purchase a property within which timeframe you can cancel the agreement without reason.

Covenant. A formal written agreement between two parties. In property, covenants usually place a restriction on how you can use or develop a property.

Development application (DA). A formal request for consent to execute a proposed development. This could include change of use of land, subdividing land, carrying out work on a building and landscaping.

Easement. A legal right to use another's land for a specific limited purpose. In other words, when someone is granted an easement, they are granted the legal right to use the property, but the legal title to the land itself remains with the owner of the land.

Joint tenants. Form of ownership of title where there are two or more people who are owners. In the event of death, the title ownership is automatically passed onto the surviving owner(s).

Marketing expenses. The expenses payable by the owner to have the property advertised in order to attract prospective tenants or buyers.

Open (open house or open for inspection). A time scheduled for prospective buyers to take a look around the property.

Owners' corporation. The name of the body which represents the building owners who share common areas of the premises.

Settlement date. The date a Contract of Sale is finalised and final payment is made.

Strata plan. The registered plan of title which shows all the boundaries of the lot and unit entitlements.

Strata property. A property with a strata title allows individual ownership of part of a property (called a 'lot' and generally an apartment or townhouse), combined with shared ownership of the 'common property' (e.g. foyers, driveways, gardens). Strata property is managed through a legal entity called the owners' corporation, body corporate or strata company.

Tenants in common. A form of ownership where each owner has a specified proportion of ownership rights in real property. Upon the death of a tenant in common, that share is transferred to the estate of the deceased tenant.

Vacant possession. The duty to ensure the property is vacant for the new owner upon the settlement of the sale.

66W waiver. The waiver form that a property purchaser may sign to waive their right to a cooling off period.

STATE GOVERNMENT BODIES

Legislation governing property sales, purchases and management is different in each state and Territory. The relevant websites are listed below.

ACT

ACT Revenue Office
www.revenue.act.gov.au/im-buying-a-new-home

New South Wales

Fair Trading
www.fairtrading.nsw.gov.au

Northern Territory

NT Government - Housing, property and land
nt.gov.au/property

Queensland

Queensland Government - Buying and selling a property
www.qld.gov.au

South Australia

SA Government - Planning and property
www.sa.gov.au

Tasmania

Consumer, building and occupational services

www.cbos.tas.gov.au

Victoria

Consumer Affairs

www.consumer.vic.gov.au

Western Australia

Department of Commerce

www.commerce.wa.gov.au/tenancy

Made in the USA
Monee, IL
14 September 2026

63198320R00114